AWFULLY GOOD MOVIES VOLUME ONE

Adventures In B-movies

Alain Elliott

CONTENTS

Title Page
Introduction
Snakes on a Plane (2006)   1
Killer Klowns From Outer Space (1988)   5
Big Ass Spider! (2013)   8
Monster from Bikini Beach (2008)   11
Ghost Shark (2013)   14
Plughead Rewired: Circuitry Man II (1994)   17
Orc Wars (AKA Dragonfyre) (2013)   20
The Deadly Bees (1966)   23
Killer Mountain (2011)   26
Sharknado (2013)   29
Blubberella (2011)   33
Octopus (2000)   35
Attack of the Sabretooth (2005)   38
Seattle Superstorm (2012)   41
Malibu Shark Attack (AKA Mega Shark In Malibu) (2009)   44
Bats (1999)   47
Pegasus Vs. Chimera (2011)   50
Snakes on a Train (2006)   53
Primal Species (AKA Carnosaur 3: Primal Species) (1996)   56
Sharknado 2: The Second One (2014)   59
Eight Legged Freaks (2002)   62

Ninja Zombies (2011)	65
Snowbeast (1977)	68
Wolf Town (2011)	70
Octopus 2: River of Fear (2001)	73
Goblin (2010)	76
Stonados (2013)	79
Monsterwolf (2010)	82
Jurassic Croc (AKA Supercroc) (2007)	85
Sharknado 3: Oh Hell No! (2015)	88
Rabbid Grannies (1988)	92
Red Water (2003)	95
Camel Spiders (2011)	98
Loch Ness Terror (2008)	101
Anacondas: Trail of Blood (2009)	104
Grabbers (2012)	107
Raiders of the Lost Shark (2015)	110
Arachnoquake (2012)	113
Piranhaconda (2012)	116
Lake Placid 2 (2007)	119
Shark Attack (1999)	122
Monstro! (2010)	125
Megalodon (2002)	127
Dead Sushi (2012)	129
Space Sharks (AKA Raging Sharks) (2005)	132
Snakehead Swamp (2014)	135
Ghostquake (AKA Haunted High) (2012)	138
Damn Sea Vampires! (2013)	141
Attack of the Vegan Zombies (2010)	144
Birdemic: Shock and Terror (2010)	147
Afterword	151

About The Author	153
Books By This Author	155

INTRODUCTION

This book is a celebration of these movies.

I want it to be clear that I love these movies and could watch this style of film forever. They are often mocked and ridiculed but there's a charm to (almost) every one of them.

Of course, I completely understand I am in the minority but there's still plenty of people that enjoy them because they keep getting made year after year. With crazier titles, crazier ideas and crazier creatures and, much much more!

I'm not sure when I started enjoying these films more than most but the first film in this book seems like a good place to start. Snakes On A Plane has a cult following like no other. Perhaps if it wasn't for Samuel L. Jackson starring and reportedly making sure the title was not changed, then the movie might have been forgotten about much sooner. Thankfully iy was not, and I'm sure it inspired many more B-movies (not just the kind of insane Snakes On A Train).

In thsi book I cover fifty movies. I could cover many more and hopefully will in the future. It's a random mix of fifty films that I hope covers a wide range of different ideas. Each as wacky and strange as the other. From Sharknadoes to giant spiders to killer klowns to zombie sushi, and so much more.

I hope you enjoy reading about these movies as much as I have enjoyed watching and writing about them. Please make sure to check out as many as these movies as you can and come back for volume two!

SNAKES ON A PLANE (2006)

'Sit back. Relax. Enjoy the fright'

Synopsis: An FBI agent takes on a plane full of deadly venomous snakes, deliberately released to kill a witness being flown from Honolulu to Los Angeles to testify against a mob boss.

Director: David R. Ellis sadly passed in 2013. He made his first film Homeward Bound II: Lost in San Francisco in 1996 and then went on to have a pretty solid career as a director. His films included Final Destination 2, Cellular, Asylum, The Final Destination and Shark Night 3D.

Cast: Samuel L. Jackson might be the biggest star to ever play a lead role in an Awfully Good movie. The story goes that he told the producers that he would not be in the movie if they went ahead and changed its title. Julianna Margulies played Carol Hathaway in E.R. and starred in 2002 horror movie Ghost Ship. More recently she has starred in the series' The Morning Show and The Good Wife. Nathan Phillips has a pretty great horror C.V. that includes Wolf Creek, Blood Vessel, Chernobyl Diaries and These Final Hours. Like many Australian actors, he also starred in Neighbours. Rachel Blanchard has appeared in several great shows including Peep Show, Fargo and Flight of the Conchords. Flex Alexander Kadeem starred in nineties hit She's All That and, 2007 remake/sequel The Hills Have Eyes II. Kenan Thompson will be known by almost everyone as one half of the comedy duo Kenan and Kel. While Keith Dallas has a decent list of genre movies and shows to his name, including iZombie, Final Destination 3 and Riding the Bullet. Horror legend Lin Shaye has starred in Dead End, the Insidious franchise, Grudge,

New Nightmare and Critters 2! Sunny Mabrey recently showed up in Cobra Kai and previously acted in Buffy spin-off Angel and xXx2: The Next Level. Terry Chen has made a name for himself in TV, including roles in Bates Motel, House of Cards, Van Helsing, Jessica Jones and The Last of Us. Elsa Pataky has played Elena in the Fast and Furious franchise. Bobby Cannavale is excellent in everything he appears in. He has starred in The Station Agent, Ant Man, The Watcher, Boardwalk Empire, Chef, Spy and Nine Perfect Strangers. David Koechner is a bit of a comedy legend starring in Anchorman, Semi-Pro, The Office and also a couple of decent horror movies including Piranha 3DD, Final Destination 5 and Krampus. There was a time when Taylor Kitsch was going to be the next big thing in Hollywood. It didn't quite work out that way but he's still had a decent career that includes starring roles in John Carter, X-Men Origins: Wolverine and True Detective.

Opening scene: After we see clips of surfers and people on a beach, we follow a guy on a dirt bike while a song called 'It's gonna be a lovely day' plays. As these credits end, the guy on the dirt bike comes across a guy hanging upside down in one of those rope traps on a tree. The ones that were really popular in nineties shows and movies. The guy is bleeding and he tells the dirt bike guy to disappear. He does as he is told but only after he watches from the bushes as the hanging guy is killed by a mafia-type guy wearing a white suit and white t-shirt, hitting him like a piñata, with a baseball bat. Messing his outfit up as it gets covered in blood.

Awfully Good Character: There's a surprisingly small amount of very entertaining characters, so I'm going to go with bad characters. There's a celebrity on board the flight, a singer by the name of Three G's. He's very stereotypical, has awful lines and he has an aversion to touching people in any way. At some point in the movie we are supposed to start liking him because he realises he's a dick and apologises to a few people after pulling a gun on them.

Awfully Good scene: Pretty early on we see a couple attempt to enter the 'Mile High Club'. Not only do they plan to have sex in the planes toilet, but also smoke some weed in there too. The weed part only seems to be in the script so that the guy takes out the smoke alarm from above them and gives a snake a place to attack them from. And attack them it does. Before killing them the snake goes for neck of guy and the bare nipple of the woman.

Awfully good line: It was always going to be the famous Samuel L. Jackson line *"Enough is enough! I have had it with these motherfucking snakes on this motherfucking plane!"*
Although if you have watched the edited PG-13 version of the film you might have heard a better one - *"I've had it with these monkey-fighting snakes on this Monday through Friday plane!"*.
I'll let you decide which one you think is better!

Other notes and scenes: We get 'snake vision' throughout the film. Which is like seeing through the eyes of a snake in night-vision. As you might have expected. The first proper kill is off-screen but it's a snake killing a cat. Lin Shaye's hair is probably worth the cost of the movie alone. A guy goes to the toilet and, as he announces it, the snake gets his dick. All the snakes and most the effects are CGI but it actually looks pretty good. There's a surprisingly large amount of blood on screen. The captain of the plane is taken out at the neck by a snake. The flight is very empty. I guess that we can be thankful for, there could have been many more casualties. The big realisation that the snakes are on board comes when lots of them drop down with the oxygen masks and cause havoc. One woman goes to use a sick bag but gets a snake in the mouth instead. Another lady gets a snake to the eye. The snakes themselves, and the movie, are quite vicious. Samuel L. Jackson uses taser to good effect on the snakes. In one of the moments of panic and people trying to run away from the snakes, one guy gets knocked to the floor and people begin to stamp over him. This leads to a surprisingly brutal and painful looking moment where a ladies high heel goes directly into his ear!
One of the air stewards manages to catch a snake with his bare hands and throws it into a nearby microwave. We see the view from inside with an explosion of blood. Baking trays work surprisingly well at batting off the snakes. Samuel L. Jackson's character thinks it is a good idea to build a 'wall' to stop the snakes getting to the part of the plane they are in. It doesn't seem like a great idea from the get go, and I was proved right.The snakes get through and it soon gets taken down. There's always a dog in danger! Unfortunately, after some near misses the tiny dog is thrown at a giant snake by

a character that gets instant karma from the giant snake that is clearly still hungry. It wraps around him and then begins to eat him, starting from the head. One of the kids gets bitten and his arm looks horrific! Decent make-up effects there. Add a fire extinguisher and lighter/spray can combo to the list of weapons that work okay versus snakes. Samuel L. Jackson and a air hostess fly the plane at one point. Not very well though. One couple attacked by lots of snakes. We see them, quite violently get spat on and bitten, over and over again. There's more brutal injuries when the stairs collapses. One guy falls and has a sharp object go into his neck. Another guy falls and another sharp object goes directly through his body as he lands on the floor.

Final scene: Samuel L. Jackson deliberately shoots a hole in two windows of the plane. The hole gets much worse though - this was the plan you see, the snakes will get sucked out as the passengers all strap themselves in and hold on. People are clinging for their lives. For a while where it doesn't seem like such a great plan! A guy that plays flight simulators on Playstation 2 is chose to pilot it home. I thought about this and checked, there wasn't many appropriate simulators on Playstation 2. When the plane lands we get a lot of actors trying to make it look like they are in a moving plane. This is clearly not as easy as it sounds! At the last moment a snake attacks our main guy but Samuel L. Jackson shoots the snake that is on his chest! It seems like a perfectly over the top ending with his pinpoint perfect shot but it turns out the guy was wearing a bullet proof vest. Not quite as risky!

Final thoughts: Not exactly the first, or a movie that started off a flurry of copycats but it's one of the most popular and well known 'Awfully Good' movies. It's also got one of the biggest casts looking back and it's good value for its money too. The snakes do not disappoint!

KILLER KLOWNS FROM OUTER SPACE (1988)

'In space, no-one can eat ice-cream!'

Synopsis: When a small town is invaded by aliens from outer space who are capturing and killing the townspeople, no one takes them seriously. Why? The aliens all look like circus clowns, use weapons that look clown-like, and all have painted on smiles.

Director: Stephen Chiodo hasn't directed many films but has special effects credits for Critters 1 and 2, Elf and Team America: World Police. Seemingly out of nowhere he popped up in 2020 for a new animated, and pretty great, Christmas movie for Netflix called Alien X-Mas.

Cast: Before this film Suzanne Snyder starred in Return of the Living Dead II and Weird Science but didn't do a whole lot after it. Grant Kramer has appeared in such greatly titled films such as Santa Claws and Leapin' Leprechauns! He also turned up in 2021 Nic Cage movie Willy's Wonderland. John Allen Nelson starred in the underrated horror sequel Feast 3 and has done a lot of TV work including Friends, 24 and Baywatch. John Vernon is probably best known for playing The Mayor in Dirty Harry. And the fantastically named Royal Dano also starred in Ghoulies 2.

Opening scene: A group of teenagers and young adults are drinking and doing the stuff they do, in a lay-by near some woodland. An ice cream van turns up with little success just as a meteor flies above and lands nearby. An old man living not far way, gets very excited at the possible tourist attraction the meteor might bring, and heads towards it with his dog. When he gets there, there's a circus tent in the middle of the woods. There's a pretty cool moment as they walk around the tent followed by a silhouette of a clown. A clown appears in a hole in the tent and steals the dog via a net. The old man is so angry that he punches the tent only to discover it is as hard as a rock. He grabs hold of the rope holding up the tent but is electrified by it. Finally a clown shoots him with some kind of ray gun.

Awfully Good character: John Vernon as the cop Curtis Mooney is an undoubted highlight. In his first scene he brings into the station two youths and is so over the top angry it's great. The two youths may or may not have been drinking in public. Regardless of that, Curtis will probably have them down for life in prison. He remains hilariously angry for most of the film. Sometimes at his younger colleague, sometimes at teenagers who haven't really done much wrong.

Awfully Good line: A film that was slightly lacking in one liners, this still amused me. *"I'm Jo-Jo the ice cream clown, we'll give you a stick, you'll give it a lick. And it'll tickle you all the way down. Ice cream, ice cream, we brought our goodies here to you! A tasty treat for while you screw! Let's take a break! Cool off those hot lips with our frozen fruity bars! Icy-wicy, fudgy-wudgy bars. And everyone's frozen delight, the lick a stick!"*

Awfully Good scene: This has to be the scene with the bikers. A gang of bikers are outside as a clown approaches them on a tricycle. Of course, they don't take him seriously and one guy asks the clown if he can have a ride on it. The clown shakes his head. So the biker asks if he can press the horn, the clown nods but the biker picks up the tricycle, throws it to the ground and destroys it! The clown disappears briefly and returns with boxing gloves on! The biker laughs in his face and asks "What are you gonna do? Knock my block off?" With that, and one punch later, the clown has punched the bikers head straight off!

Other notes and scenes: Killer Klowns has a lot to write about. The 'ray' guns the clowns use wrap the humans in a sort of cotton candy (or candy floss) cocoon. They also have another type of gun - a popcorn gun! It just fires popcorn at people. At first, this doesn't seem that great but much later into the film we discover that the popcorn turns into snake clowns! Yes really. The clowns soon start cocooning everyone in town. Knocking on peoples doors as pizza delivery clowns, chocolate delivery clowns, and more. There's one car chase scene, except the clown doesn't have a car. He just sits in that position and goes along using his feet as lights. One clown makes some shadow puppets on a wall, only for the dinosaur shadow to eat some nearby onlookers. One of the cops does discover a way to kill the clowns. If you shoot at, or destroy their nose, then the whole clowns body just kind of explodes! Sometimes, instead of a cocoon of candy floss, one girl is shot into some kind of balloon, trapped inside. Cream pies from outer space are a lot more deadly it seems too because when a security guy is attacked with several of them, they melt him to the ground. We also get to see some female clowns with inflating breasts!

Final scene: The finale goes on for a while. The two main male characters, a boyfriend and ex of the main female character, are searching for her. They first witness an overweight clown drinking from one of the cocoons. They shoot him and he explodes. Next they shoot the balloon to let the girl escape. The three of them are then chased by several clowns (or Klowns I guess). They slide down a pole and through a tunnel of perfectly normal looking balloons and through a fairground-like maze, finally opening several doors on each other until they go through a tiny door. But then they are surrounded by clowns, only to be saved by two friends driving the ice cream van through the tent. But before they can escape, a giant evil clown descends from above on strings. The giant clown starts destroying the van, throwing it aside and starting a huge explosion. The clown then picks up the cop in one hand, while the couple manage to escape. As the circus tent begins to fly away, the cop manages to burst the giant clowns nose with his badge. Leading to an even bigger explosion of the whole tent! Somehow, the cop survives via the ridiculous looking clown car. Also with him are the two ice cream van drivers who survived each explosion by hiding in the freezer compartment. Everything I've mentioned is as ridiculous as it sounds.

Final thoughts: Killer Klowns From Outer Space is fantastic. Perhaps the perfect Awfully Good film! How it got made, I'll never know. But the cheap effects and sets are something you have to see. A film so ridiculous you can't help but love it.

BIG ASS SPIDER! (2013)

'10 stories tall, 1 huge appetite.'

Synopsis: A giant alien spider escapes from a military lab and rampages the city of Los Angeles. When a massive military strike fails, it is up to a team of scientists and one clever exterminator to kill the creature before the city is destroyed.

Director: Mike Mendez has gone from strength to strength since Big Ass Spider! He followed up with a super fun segment in the criminally under seen Tales of Halloween, and then went into the even more ridiculous Lavalantula. In 2016 he directed Dolph Lundgren in the very entertaining Don't Kill It. Unfortunately it was another six years for his next movie, the well received horror, Satanic Hispanics (soon coming to Shudder!)

Cast: Greg Grunberg plays the main role as Alex the exterminator. Before Big Ass Spider he was best known for his roles in Alias and Heroes. But, since then he has had roles in Star Wars: The Force Awakens and The Rise of Skywalker, Star Trek Beyond, The Flash, Castle Rock, Satanic Hispanics and Spielberg's latest The Fableman's. Clare Kramer is the lead female role. She hasn't actually been in that much but was of course awesome as Glory in Buffy the Vampire Slayer and like Grunberg, also starred in Tales of Halloween. I feel like she should have had a bigger career! Lombardo Boyar is the other main guy. He was seen in Dawn of the Planet of the Apes. I see a link here, as he also acted in Tales of Halloween and Satanic Hispanics. He also did some pretty high profile voice work in Pixar's Coco. Lin Shaye appears briefly in an early scene. Horror fans will best know her for the Insidious franchise, and the lesser known but great Dead End. Still regularly working in good films, Shaye has appeared in the last few years in films such as Anderson Falls, Grudge and Ouija: Origin of Evil. Ray Wise is known for a million things, maybe to most people for Twin Peaks or to horror fans Jeepers Creepers 2 or the aforementioned Dead End alongside Shaye. He's great in Digging Up the Marrow. And finally, director of many

Troma films Lloyd Kaufman gets a small cameo.

Opening scene: The first scene plays out like a music video. Music plays as we see our 'hero' Alex open his eyes and look around, while in slow motion around him there's people panicking, fires and explosions. The camera finally pans around as we see a big ass spider climbing a sky scraper with helicopters flying and then crashing around it until the title screen appears.

Awfully Good performance: I'm going to have to mention two here. Patrick Bauchau plays Lucas, an expert of the spider who just continuously gives out facts about the spider to the military and tells them to do something about it. He's never much help and the military give up on him eventually.
My second one is Lombardo Boyar as Jose, who is just plain great! He has some great lines and his comic timing and delivery are perfect, as are his mannerisms.

Awfully Good line: In reply to Jose's queries on the spider, Alex replies with **"What I saw was 20 inches and black"**. Jose chuckles like the rest of us. Childish humour that will usually get a laugh.

Awfully Good Scene: The spider goes on a rampage through the local park. There's girls in bikinis playing volleyball (because, of course there is), people running in panic getting stabbed and sprayed by the spiders web and reeled in. Blood goes everywhere, it's alot of fun!

Other notes and scenes: Well any time the spider attacks is a highlight. Including a guy being grabbed from the floor while the spider hides in a tree. The car chase involving Alex and Jose being chased by the spider is great. The interaction between the two is funny and Alex answers the phone in full 'phone voice' for his company. Soon after this we see a great slow motion jump of the spider over the military while they shoot at it. Jose running full pace at the spider while shooting also got a laugh. A man gets ripped in half at one point! The news report scenes were nicely shot, as were the scenes of the spider crawling through the streets of the city, destroying buildings. At times, reminiscent of Godzilla. There's also a funny scene with Alex and Jose in a lift, going to meet the spider on top of the sky scraper. They have a quick sing and dance to there own spider killing song. The scene before the final scene involves the spider being shot down from the sky scraper.

Final scene: The spiders demise. After Alex manages to dodge the spiders attempts at striking him, Jose throws him the bazooka, which he manages to fire up the spiders butt, exploding it into pieces.

Final thoughts: Big Ass Spider! is just a whole lot of fun. Delivers exactly what you would expect with the title but with comedy that is actually funny. Some people won't like the CGI spider but it generally looked good and worked for the film. I wholly recommend Big Ass Spider!

MONSTER FROM BIKINI BEACH (2008)

'It's a cool, retro dance party from Hell!'

Synopsis: One man dares suspect a truth too terrifying to believe, while a crooked cop tries to cash in on the score of a lifetime! Thrown together by destiny, the two find themselves locked in the final bloody battle to defend Bikini Beach.

Director: Unfortunately I haven't seen any of Darin Wood's other films, because based on their titles I'd love them. They are, Curse of the Golden Skull, Planet of the Vampire Woman and Badass Monster Killer.

Cast: There are several actors in this film that had appeared in less than three films when this was made. David Ainsworth, Betty Chiang, Sid Garcia-Heberger, Bethany Hidden and Bryce Marck all fall into the category of this being their first film. Several of the actors worked on this early in their careers but haven't worked any 'major films since. Such as West Ramsey (Mondo Sacramento, Sawtooth, in which he played Bigfoot!), Galen Howard (Reel Evil, Children of Sorrow). A couple of actors have have had decent careers since Monster From Bikini Beach. Liesel Hanson has starred in Happy Hunting and Tales of Halloween. Galen Howard has appeared in Slayers, Deathcember and a couple of episodes of Agents of S.H.E.I.L.D. and The Book of Boba Fett. While Laura Megan Stahl has made a career out of mainly voice work, including games such as Fire Emblem: Engage, Octopath Traveller II and God of War: Ragnorak.

Opening scene: Unsurprisingly, things open with some girls in bikinis dancing on a beach. The music is hilariously bad, and then the monster attacks! The monster is not CGI but an actual outfit some guy obviously had to wear. But it's pretty massive and looks kind of awful, kind of awesome all at the same time. Anyway, the monster cuts open one guy, whose intestines fall everywhere and then impressively cuts off a girls bikini top and drags her away.

Awfully Good character: I will have to go with a character almost entirely because of her name. Honey 'Boom Boom' Stacks. She's a ditzy dancer who is dating the mobster at least three times her age.

Awfully Good line: And from Honey Boom Boom Stacks came this classic line. *'"I hate crime.........so much!"*. It might not sound like much but the delivery of the line is thankfully, Awfully Good. This only just beat the line *"This creepy place is giving me the creeps!"*

Awfully Good scene: A blonde stripper runs into two drug dealers down a back alley and a fight soon ensues. All are in possession of knives but the stripper is surprisingly good with her kicks and fends off the two guys for a short while. But when she loses her knife it seems she's in trouble. Enter, the monster! It bites one guys head clean off, leaving a body spurting with blood from the neck. It then quickly kills the other guy, with guts and intestines going everywhere. The scene closes as the monster approaches the stripper.

Other notes and scenes: The monster attacks are an obvious highlight. It attacks three bikini clad girls in a dingy. It eats a couple of girls when they fall out of the tiny boat, blood and gore goes everywhere. The remaining girl gets to the beach injured, but is dragged back into the water when the monster grabs her via her intestines (intestines do a lot of work in this movie). A crazy drunk woman who is dressed in the most over the top outfit, tells our two main characters about the monster, just before she is killed by it. The viewer only gets to see blood splatter on the wall. At one crime scene, the monster did leave a 'foot print'. There's a very long and pointless shower scene with one woman. The monster then hilariously attacks her in the shower but this turns out to be a dream. A body is thrown off the bridge and into a river at one point. This body is clearly a dummy. We meet a new couple almost halfway through the film, in this scene the girl seems to be wrestling a green blanket which i think is supposed to be a alligator. My favourite image has to be the monster carrying a girl away. There's a nice line about the Scooby-Doo villains always being a man in a scary suit....which is then followed by a Scooby-Doo-like chase scene.

So much seems to happen in this film, even slow motion gun fights, which includes a Awfully Good fall into a swimming pool. At least one more guy is decapitated by the monster. Before we get to the last scene, the monster enters a club that is holding a Go-Go-athon! He runs through the club tearing people apart, attacking and eating them. It shows it's skill of ripping the bikini tops off of girls in one quick swipe. Because I realise I haven't mentioned this, the monster is trying to find the perfect human woman to mate with. I'm not sure I want to even think about how that would work.

Final scene: The monster leaves the club and obviously ends up on the beach. Alot of girls start screaming and usually end up topless, covered in blood and guts and eventually dead. The old detective of the film ends up one on one with the monster. The gun shots aren't really working but luckily for him he has a bag full of cocaine to use. I'm not sure why but this does work. He throws it into the monsters mouth and shoots at it. The monster spurts out some green gunk and slowly dies. The camera pans around the beach as the film ends with bodies sprawled everywhere.

Final thoughts: There's not much more else you could ask for from a monster B-movie! I loved Monster From Bikini Beach. The monster itself is brilliant. I much prefer a 'ridiculous but great looking guy in a suit' style monster, than a cheap CGI one. The whole film is very tongue in cheek and knows exactly what kind of movie it is. And perhaps the best thing about it is that it is FREE to watch on Youtube! So sit back and enjoy.

GHOST SHARK (2013)

*'It's a shark that's a ghost.
Need anything else?'*

Synopsis: When rednecks on a fishing trip kill a great white shark, its spirit comes back for revenge, and soon turns its sights on the town of Smallport.

Director: Perhaps better known for his acting work which features roles in I Love You Phillip Morris, Focus and the show Banshee, Griff Furst nonetheless has had an interesting directorial career also. Although he hasn't made a movie since 2018, he has made Lake Placid 3, Swamp Shark, Arachnoquake, Ragin Cajun Redneck Gators, Shark Shock, Nightmare Shark and the surprisingly good Cold Moon.

Cast: Mackenzie Rosman starred in a long running TV series called 7th Heaven as a child but Ghost Shark seems to be her last ever role of any note. Dave Randolph-Mayhem Davis (yes that's his middle name, although disappointingly, he seems to be going by Dave Davis now) has had lots of small roles, including one in True Detective, and he's had trouble in water before in SnakeHead Swamp. Most recently showing up in The Vigil and Emancipation. Sloane Coe also appeared in SnakeHead Swamp, 2014's horror Devil's Due and Shark Island but nothing since 2015. Jaren Mitchell has had small roles in several high profile shows and movies, including True Detective, True Blood, Now You See Me, 21 Jump Street and American Horror Story. Recently he has had decent roles in The Purge TV show and Your Honor, aswell as the highly entertaining 2018 movie End Trip.
SnakeHead Swamp and True Detective seem to link several actors in this film.

Opening scene: We start with two hill-billy types, a Father and daughter, who I think are attempting to win a fishing competition by catching the largest fish. Just as they are about to get the fish, a shark comes jumping out of the water and bites the fish in half!

Now very unhappy with the shark, they decide they must kill it, obviously. So with a combination of guns, hot sauce and a grenade they do manage to blow it up. But, as the title suggests this isn't the end for the shark and after it enters some magical cave returning with a blue transparent glow and goes straight to killing the father and daughter. The deaths aren't very graphic but a bit of blood is splashed about the place.

Awfully Good performance: Richard Moll (House, Jingle All The Way, Slay Belles) as Finch the lighthouse keeper is alot of fun. He's a bit crazy and generally just does alot of shouting while trying to explain the mysteries of the Ghost Shark and its history.

Awfully Good line: And Richard Moll gets this too. On the discovery of the dead shark he utters just two words *"Judas Priest"*. Yep, the heavy metal/rock band was the first thing that came to his mind.

Awfully Good scene: As the shark can enter any kind of water, big or small, this was quite a hard pick. But one scene for me stood out. A guy takes a drink from a water cooler. A few seconds later he is moving around in pain, blood coming from his mouth. Then, as he stands up straight, his body slowly splits in half vertically as the ghost shark itself appears moving up through the body and then completely out before disappearing. Not only is it just an absolutely insane scene, I thought the effects for the body splitting (practical with models, not CGI) looked really good.

Other notes and scenes: Remember, this Ghost Shark can appear anywhere that there is water! Obviously the death scenes are the highlights here but there are a couple of other interesting moments. At the start of the film a girl is swimming from the shark when she sees someone she knows on a jet-ski. She shouts at him something about the shark and he acts a bit confused as she jumps on the jet-ski. They could have both rode off then and there but she thought she would push the guy into the water to his almost certain death and ride off on her own!

There's a scene at the end of the film where a fire alarm goes off in the library. This sets off the sprinkler system which, for me, flooded the library way to quickly! They obviously hadn't thought about the chances of a ghost shark.

But yes, the death scenes are generally great. When you first discover that the shark can go almost anywhere, it comes up from what is basically a puddle of water to bite a man completely in half. The local teenagers then have a pool party, something the shark was hoping for I'm sure. A cocky teenager jumps off the board flipping into the pool. But before he even hits the water, the shark leaps out of the pool swallowing him in one. Well that's not quite true, as the guys head flies off and lands on another guys bottle top. Next up is a plumber. He's happily working away under someone's kitchen sink but of course there's a leak. And that's all the shark needs as he leaps from the tiny pipes and drags the man to his death. Even children aren't safe from ghost shark. Once happily playing on a water slide in their garden, the shark enjoys a ride and in the process gobbles up some children! A child also witnesses a blood covered shark attack too. Seeing bikini clad women offering to wash cars, a young teenager drives, I assume his parents car, to get washed. But his happiness is soon over when the car is splattered with the blood of the women when ghost shark comes splashing through the water. My favourite child death scene (that's not a line I thought I'd ever write) comes when the main characters enter a 'bad' area of town. Some not very tough looking kids start threatening them. But unfortunately for the kids they are playing near a fire hydrant that is spraying out water. Ghost shark does not miss opportunities like this and chomps in half several of the children in one quick moment. Of course there is an entertaining toilet death scene too.

Final Scene: The end is a bit disappointing considering everything that has gone on before it. It's raining (obviously) and the shark threatens a bit until it is blown up in the mysterious cave it was created in. A slight let down.

Final thoughts: Ghost Shark is a whole lot of fun and makes a very entertaining watch. Right up there with the Sharknado films, perhaps even better. I really like Ghost Shark.

PLUGHEAD REWIRED: CIRCUITRY MAN II (1994)

'Plug in, again!'

Synopsis: In the backdrop of Earth's polluted future a female FBI agent removes Danner, a pleasure android from an asylum in order to coerce him into helping her hunt down the criminal psychopath Plughead.

Directors: I assume the two directors are brothers, Robert and Steven Lovy. Robert never directed again, while Steven directed the first Circuitry Man and then ten years after this sequel directed a film called Mix.

Cast: Dennis Christopher has had an interesting career with films such as Django Unchained, Chariots of Fire and many TV shows on his C.V. including playing Eddie in the original It. Nicholas Worth starred in Swamp Thing, Darkman, Barb Wire and Don't Answer The Phone! Traci Lords has starred in many films including the excellent horror film Excision, Blade and the almost certainly Awfully Good Sharkansas Women's Prison Massacre. Paul Wilson is best known for his role as Paul Krapence in TV show Cheers. Vernon Wells is another busy actor still at 78. Previously he's appeared in Commando and Weird Science. He starred in ten films in 2023, so he's showing no sign of slowing down in 2024. Deborah Shelton starred in 2006's The Strange Case of Dr. Jekyll and Mr. Hyde. Jim Meltzler appeared in TV show Dexter as well as LA Confidential.

Opening scene: After a short on screen worded intro, we see a woman on an operation table. She is telling the people around her to plug her head to Plughead's head before the F.B.I. arrive. They do as they are told and the two start 'talking' telepathically. Plughead tells the woman he will help her become pregnant (I'm not exactly sure how other than the obvious) even though she can't have children, if she helps him.

Awfully Good character: I'm going with two characters. Leech (Christopher) and Rock (Worth). They are the George and Lennie of the film and are clearly influenced by them two characters. Rock playing the simpleton controlled by Leech. Their relationship is a highlight of the film and actually has some good moments despite a dodgy script. Rock being in love with a rock being one of the stupider ideas. But the chemistry between the two is pretty good and at times fun.

Awfully Good line: There's a few to choose from but I'm going with *"Sucking dust like a $10 whore on speed!"* Lovingly said by Leech.

Awfully Good scene: The sex scene has to have this honour! Despite not liking each other much through the movie, characters Kyle and Danner seemingly fall in love all of a sudden while riding a horse. They actually don't leave the horse to start stripping off but thankfully they do to have sex. It's all accompanied by the cheesiest of music and doesn't last long.

Other notes and scenes: The story revolves around Kyle getting 'pleasure android' Danner to help her defeat the evil Plughead. But Plughead is involving Kyle in his plan to sell longevity chips to people around the world so he can then control them. I'm not sure these chips are worth getting as they extend life by just ten years but Plughead thinks they'll be popular. Plughead initially looks like a character from Facejacker. We are introduced to two 1950's looking cops (this is set in the future) by them bumping into another cop while he just happens to be holding some explosives. This plays out like some awful skit on a comedy sketch show. This comedy cop duo I think are after Plughead and require a ridiculous looking car that travels 1000 miles a minute, to get to him. The inside of the car is even more ridiculous and cheap looking. There's a moment when Kyle and Danner look like they dig up an arm and eat it. It's actually a big carrot. I think. Of course there is a bit of cheap C.G.I. The two lovers acquire pairs of sand shoes which are definitely not needed and seemingly slows them down. Especially when they attempt to run in them. Danner gets shot a couple of times and comes out with the great line "I've never been shot twice in the same day. Come to think of it. Never once." About halfway through the film the film-makers decide some people need something extra to keep watching. So Kyle loses her jacket and has a low cut top to show her cleavage off some more. Despite his initial appearance, Plughead does come across as quite an imposing figure. Not unlike

Pinhead in several ways. Although it nearly disappears when he arrives through smoke like a contestant on Stars in Their Eyes. As the film goes on his look gets much scarier and the make-up actually looks pretty good. Rock is seemingly beaten to death through a window while a heartbroken Leech looks on. But he comes back. One of the highlights involves a safe randomly falling on a guy as he is about to attack. It then opens to show lots of money for the two. Although I'm not sure they have the cash by the end of the film.

Final scene: Of course, it all comes down to Danner saving the captured Kyle from Plughead. We go inside Plughead's mind with effects that look like a painted background. He attacks Danner when a wire comes out from his split forehead in a quite cool looking and gruesome moment. But Danner plugs it into himself so they both enter his mind. His mind consists of a lot of white and him and Kyle walking towards each other with candles and then kissing. This makes Plughead exclaim "What are you gonna do? Kill me with your love?" And, well yes, that is what they are gonna do. Plughead spontaneously combusts! But then the fire disappears. I didn't understand that bit. But it doesn't matter because a few seconds later, the couples love just makes his whole body and head explode in a one fantastic second! The forgotten cop duo are then shown messing about in their car. They never appear at the desired location and I'm not quite sure why they were in the film. The film ends with Leech and a blonde woman who I haven't really mentioned, falling in love. Danner and Kyle walk in front hand in hand and Rock is in love with his rock still but now no longer a mute and reciting some poetry.

Final thoughts: Plughead Rewired: Circuitry Man II is fantastically cheesy and Awfully Good. More of a sci-fi than horror but it's hard not to enjoy. I will soon be checking out the first film.

ORC WARS (AKA DRAGONFYRE) (2013)

'The battle for our world begins'

Synopsis: A battle-weary ex-Special Forces Operative buys a ranch in remote American West to flee from the world, only to encounter a strange series of trespassers, including a beautiful elf princess, a Native American mystic, and Orcs. When the Orcs invade his property, John must give up his isolation to become a hero before the Orcs unleash their dragon god on our world.

Director: Kohl Glass has directed has at least two other intriguing sounding movies - You May Now Kill the Bride and Josie Jane: Kill the Babysitter.

Cast: Another interestingly named person is in the lead role. Rusty Joiner. They also appeared in Dodgeball and Resident Evil: Extinction. More interesting names keep coming, because the main female role is played by Masiela Lusha who also appeared in Blood: The Last Vampire, Sharknado 4, 5 & 6 and an Alanis Morissette video - that's quite the variety! Wesley John doesn't have many film roles to his name but his first was in The Scorpion King. Isaac C. Singleton Jr has done a lot of voice work, including Thanos in the Marvel animated universe and Sagat in several Streetfighter games. He has appeared in a couple of big shows too - Agents of S.H.E.I.L.D. and The Mandolorian included. Maclain Nelson is no stranger to Awfully Good films, starring in Orcs!, Dragon Hunter and Dragon Warriors. He now seems to be concentrating on producing. Adam Johnson also appeared in Orcs! and Dragon Hunter as well as Adam Green's Frozen and Brooklyn Nine-Nine. Claire Niederpruem can be added to the Orcs! List, as well as Zombie Hunter with Danny Trejo, while currently making a living through Christmas movies. Jake Van Wagoner is best known for directing and producing. His shows include Show Offs (also starring Maclain Nelson) and Impractical Jokers. Rocky Meyers has worked on Lucifer, Quantum Leap and Magnum P.I. all in the last few years.

Opening scene: There's three people running from something in a forest. It's orcs! They attack and kill one guy, an arrow takes down another guy and the girl is told to "look for the wizard". The girl runs from the many orcs and into a cave entrance that is some kind of portal. She runs into the wizard who then proceeds to take out the orcs with a load of guns. Four guns in fact! Despite killing off all the orcs, the wizard also dies as the opening credits pop up.

Awfully Good character: Whitefeather. Not only does he have a pretty awful native American name but he's blind, and still awesome at sword fighting. He battles off many orcs with his sword and has the best line in the film (see below). Unfortunately towards the end of the film, there are one too many orcs and they kill him. Oh, he also drives a tank truck thing with a little help on the directions.

Awfully Good line: When Whitefeather is injured, they unwrap the bandages over his eyes. The holes where his eyes should be are a shocking image to the other characters. They remain in silence for a few seconds to which Whitefeather says *"Know need to say anything. I already know I'm damn good looking."* It's perhaps unfair to call it Awfully Good because it got a legitimate laugh from me.

Awfully Good scene: Actually just one small moment. A dragon enters the fight at one point. He can breath fire, fly and, I expect, eat any human it wants. But in this moment, I'm sure it headbutts one of the characters.

Other notes and scenes: The big CGI dragon appears early on in the film but then goes missing until the last fifteen minutes. The orcs actually look pretty cool. I guess they are probably men in masks rather than make-up but they still look good. The main guy is a former army member so luckily he knows how to kill things. He's also very muscular so obviously opts to do D.I.Y. topless. At first the orcs fight him off easily but he finds a hammer and screwdriver to start killing. Actually, the weapons must have just gave him confidence because he doesn't seem to need them. Throughout the first half of the film he seems more bothered about the orcs being on his land than anything else. One great line had the orcs ask a guy "Are you the wizard?" his reply? "No, I'm adopted". I'm not sure how that mattered either or maybe I didn't get the joke. The girl in the film, an elf, is actually pretty nifty with knives and a sword. Killing off many orcs throughout the film, but she sometimes seems to put herself in trouble by jumping at the orcs instead of keeping her distance. At one point an orc is tied to a chair and 'tortured' with a taser gun. This somehow becomes comical when the orc 'cries' in pain. I think it's the orcs odd and amusing voice. The orcs often have a glorious and very funny bemused and surprised look on their faces during the film. The elf girl, who is from another world and never lived in our world, soon picks up how to drive a quad bike and use guns. The estate agent woman who sold the house to the army guy, reappears during the end of the film and is luckily a dab hand at using a sniper gun. Normal guns aren't enough it seems, because the orcs are soon taken down by the aforementioned tank-like truck. Or truck-like tank. I'm not sure what the difference is. It has a manned gun on top to. The orcs counter that with a giant catapult. The estate agent is suddenly shot out of nowhere. An orc has picked up a gun! I guess guns are easy to use because everyone can use them without being shown. The dragon then comes back when the orcs are not doing so well. The orcs just stand back and cheer on the dragon while it aims its flames at the army guy and his friends.

Final scene: Army guy is down. But he dreams his old army buddies are there to pick him up. Meanwhile, the elf girl is ready to be sacrificed by the orcs and their leader of sorts, a girl-orc thing covered in white clothing. The girl is chained to a post but Whitefeather returns and this is where he eventually dies. Army guy manages to kill off the dragon with his new sword. A bazooka didn't quite do the job. He then stabs the white woman but that doesn't kill her. It takes elf girl to shoot her in the head. One orc has survived and vowels to return and kill them all! Surprisingly, elf girl and army guy don't get it on but go their separate ways.

Final thoughts: I thought Orc Wars was actually massively entertaining in the most ridiculous way. It has action from start to finish, it's funny at times, even if it's not supposed to be, it has awful CGI but it's still fun and easy to watch.

THE DEADLY BEES (1966)

'Hives of horror'

Synopsis: Trouble strikes when an exhausted pop singer, sent on a vacation to a farm, realizes that the farm's owner raises deadly bees.

Director: Director Freddie Francis went on to direct some other cool films, including Tales From the Crypt, The Creeping Flesh, Son of Dracula and The Ghoul (starring Peter Cushing).

Cast: Suzanna Leigh also appeared in Son of Dracula, as well as Lust For a Vampire. Strangely, after not working since 1978, she starred in a film in 2015 called Grace of the Father but sadly died in 2017. Frank Finlay is a quite well known British actor, who has appeared in Lifeforce, The Pianist and the 1984 version of A Christmas Carol. Guy Dolman's biggest role was in the James Bond film Thunderball. Catherine Finn is best known for her horror roles in The Creeping Flesh and Torture Garden. Brilliantly, all of her photos on her IMDb page are gruesome ones from Deadly Bees! John Harvey has 164 acting credits to his name including the nicely titled 'The Satanic Rites of Dracula'. He also starred in Doctor Who, Some Mothers Do 'Ave 'Em and Rentaghost. Michael Ripper can top him though with 246 credits! Including, The Mummy, Revenge of Frankenstein and Dracula Has Risen From the Grave. The strangest appearance in The Deadly Bees is Ronnie Wood, playing in the band at the beginning of the film.

Opening scene: Not much of note here. A bee keeper is doing his job, lots of bees flying around. A horror style score plays as the credits start.

Awfully Good character: I enjoyed Catherine Finn the most in her role as Mary Hargrove. She plays the wife of Ralph (Doleman). She is generally miserable and fed up with life. She believes her husband is cheating on her and she never seems to want to leave the chair she is sitting in. The bees soon give her an early demise from her life.

Awfully Good line: One exchange of words fits nicely here. When paperwork is needed to be found in a home to prove a character is using deadly bees, this conversation happens:
"He must keep records somewhere"
"Where?"
"Oh, he did seem annoyed when I went near his desk the other day"
"Well he must keep them there"

Some fantastic detective work I'm sure you'll agree.

Awfully Good scene: After the death of her dog, Mary tries to take revenge on the bees! She chucks petrol on the hives, and despite her husband attempting to stop her, she sets fire to them. Ralph then gets a hose and starts to put the fire out. Only the hose is a bit useless and it seems to take a lot longer than it should. The flames went up very quickly. He does eventually put them out though, using his feet to stamp out the last of them.

Other notes and scenes: The island the farm is on and where the film is set, is called Seagull Island. I have no idea why this makes me laugh, but it does. The first time we see the bees attack is when they kill the family dog. The dog barks a lot and then the camera cuts away as we hear the dog squeal until it is then found lying on its side. I thought the special effects for the bees actually looked okay. Especially considering this is over 50 years old. The close-ups of actual bees helps to. Mary's death for instant, looked quite harrowing, as bees cover her face and she goes down screaming. One of the characters can hypnotise bees!! Which actually sounds better than what it is. Which is, just playing a sound to them that stops them doing anything. A verdict of 'death by misadventure' got me interested enough to look it up. For those like me that don't know it's 'death that is primarily attributed to an accident which occurred due to a dangerous risk which was taken voluntarily'. Like any film of this type, the main female character had to be attacked while just wearing her underwear. Then, when trapped in a small room, she takes the strange step of setting fire to a towel to ward off the bees. While I said the effects for the bees wasn't too bad, when the camera starts to move, it goes a bit downhill. There's a flashback scene and then a scene in which the main villain explains why he's done what he has done, relaying everything that happens in the film. And it covers it all in a couple of minutes. Could save you time if you don't fancy watching the full hour and twenty minutes. There's a twist that is kind of obvious but I liked it.

Final scene: The local pub owner spies on who he thinks owns the deadly bees. He is then attacked by the bees but quickly saved by the person he suspected. The film's lead character Vicki Robbins, is now trapped with the villain. She takes an age to even attempt to escape but eventually throws an ornament at him. She then sees off the bees with smoke but accidentally sets the house on fire. She is of course saved though, while I assume the villain burnt to death with his bees.

Final thoughts: The Deadly Bees isn't as tongue in cheek as the more modern Awfully Good films but I still quite enjoyed it. Some poor acting and poor special effects can't stop it being at least a little bit fun.

KILLER MOUNTAIN (2011)

*'On top of the World, there's
no-one to save you'*

Synopsis: A group of mountain climbers disappear while climbing the Himalayas in the 1950s. In the present, another group takes the same route and also disappears. A shady rich man hires a professional mountaineer and some scientists to find them.

Director: Sheldon Wilson is no stranger to Awfully Good films. He's also directed Shark Killer, Snowmageddon, Mega Cyclone and Stickman (a horror movie apparently, not the children's cartoon).

Cast: Emmanuelle Vaugier has starred in episodes of Two and Half Men and Lost Girl, as well as Saw II. Aaron Douglas has appeared in The Returned, Hemlock Grove and The Killing. He played chief Galen Tyrol in 67 episodes of Battlestar Galactica and Colonel Nickson in the 2019 Van Helsing series. Paul Campbell is another TV star, another for Battlestar Galactica (as Billy Keikeya). About 75% of Campbells work in the last six years seems to be TV Christmas movies. Andrew Airlie has done a lot of TV work, including Bates Motel. He played Mr. Grey in Fifty Shades of Grey, which I assumed would be the lead role but when I looked it up, it seems there's a whole family of Grey's in that movie. Yan-Kay Crystal Lowe has been seen in films such as Final Destination 3, Hot Tub Time Machine, Wrong Turn 2: Dead End, Black Christmas 2006 and Yeti: Curse of the Snow Demon. Torrance Coombs has done TV work on The Tudors and one episode of Supernatural. Zak Santiago is no stranger to Awfully good films such as Chupacabra vs the Alamo, as well as the American remake of The Eye. As for TV, he played Cross in Dirk Gently's Holistic Detective Agency and a prison guard for six episodes of the wonderful Peacemaker show. Robin Nielsen appeared in the adaptation of Stephen King's Riding the Bullet. Byron Lawson has appeared in Awfully Good classic Snakes on a Plane. Dale Wilson has done a lot of voice work but also starred in Hellraiser: Hellseeker. While Mig Macario played Bashful in the Once Upon a Time series.

Opening scene: It's Bhutan (somewhere in the Himalayas), 1954. We see tents on a snowy mountain and someone is injured. They are 10,000 + feet up and trying to call for help when some kind of monster attacks! It eats one guy in a split second and quickly disappears.

Awfully Good character: There's no quick witted character or anything like that, so I'm gonna go with the monster. It's apparently a Druk. I'd never heard of it, but it's a mythical creature that looks a bit like a dragon with no wings. At first it looks like a giant worm because we don't get to see all of it and it's 'babies' are just big worms. It doesn't look as cool as the cover would suggest but at least it's original.

Awfully Good line: Without context, this line is nothing. But when things are going wrong and one character says ***"I'm getting out of here"***, I'm not sure exactly where he was going to go. The group were 20,000 feet up a mountain with the helicopter they came up with crashed and of no use. He was stuck where he was.

Awfully Good scene: The helicopter has crashed but out of nowhere we see the main part of it is still intact but stationary on the cliff edge, with the pilot still inside. He is joined by a couple of people to try and save him and they are connected to rope to stop them falling. All of a sudden the helicopter just falls off the edge of the mountain. There was no reason for this, it was wobbling over the edge. But unfortunately for the pilot he goes down with it.

Other notes and scenes: Helicopters are clearly expensive to hire for a film because many of these films I watch have poor CGI helicopters. Killer Mountain is one of them. When the CGI monster attacks, it's not the best looking shot of the film. And when it looks like this helicopter will crash, the guy in charge is clearly more worried about his vehicle being out of use, than his pilot dying. Two other things that mysteriously fall off of the mountain are a bag off of someone's back and a helicopter tyre that went the same way as the helicopter. One of the several groups of people in the movie are looking for the mythical city of Shambhala. Another thing I learnt about from this film.
The Druk manages to grab a girl from behind at one point with two guys

watching on. They either did not see the giant monster or chose not to tell her. There's actually some pretty decent practical effects and one or two decent looking stunts in Killer Mountain. I have a soft spot for practical effects even if they are not so great. There's also another reason for searching the mountain. There might be a cure for cancer up there. I'm not sure why but it seems possible. The first blood we see is from the baby monster worm things, that we then discover have blood that heals wounds (and maybe cancer?!). Two characters are then eaten by these worms. What you think is the end sequence doesn't actually end up being it. The final two survivors escape out of the monsters cave and set a trigger for an explosion that seemingly kills the monsters. To which one survivor says "Lets get the frack out of here". Next up are some other people put to there knees and shot from behind. So violent murder is okay here but swearing not so much.

Final scene: As you probably guessed, at least one monster survives. The army (who showed up at some point. Or just someone that looked like an army) try shooting at the Druk but it doesn't go so well. One guy shoots some lights above him which then fall on to him and set him on fire. As he's run about on fire, one of the survivors has an idea! He pours petrol nearby, so when he falls over, it starts an explosion that kills the Druk. The film is over but not before one more great line, "Holy moly!".

Final thoughts: Killer Mountain takes itself far too seriously but is somewhat enjoyable. The Druk is original and kind of cool looking at times and the whole film is ridiculous enough to be fun for the most part.

SHARKNADO (2013)

'Enough said!'

Synopsis: When a freak hurricane swamps Los Angeles, nature's deadliest killer rules sea, land, and air as thousands of sharks terrorize the waterlogged populace.

Director: Since the first movie Anthony C. Ferrante went on to direct the five Sharknado sequels. His last three movies don't sound quite as exciting though, with Nix, Crown Prince of Christmas and Butch Cassidy and the Wild Bunch.

Cast: Tara Reid will always be known for her roles in the American pie franchise but horror fans will remember her in Urban Legend too. Since the first Sharknado she has worked A LOT and mainly in similar low budget movies. Her only appearances in 2023 were the TV series Ghosts and the films Of Things Past and Bloodthirst. Despite leading all of the Sharknado films, Ian Zeiring hasn't done a whole lot else of note. The highlights of his career are probably the many many episodes of Beverly Hills 90210 as Ronnie Robertson and his recent appearances in the Swamp Thing series. John Heard had a long and pretty distinguished career but will always be known for his role as Kevin's dad in the first two Home Alone movies. Jaason Simmons has had a shortlived TV and film acting career but he starred in Frankenstein Reborn!, 3-Headed Shark Attack and, in Baywatch as Logan Fowler. Julie McCullough appeared in The Blob and after looking at her IMDb page I discovered there is a mockumentary on the Sharknado movies called 'Sharknado: Heart of Sharkness. McCullough's last two movies were A Karate Christmas Miracle and A Wrestling Christmas Miracle. Marcus Choi has had small roles in Luke Cage, Can You Ever Forgive Me? and Isn't It Romantic. In the same year of Sharknado, Israel Saez de Miguel also appeared in Jurassic Attack. Aswell as the Sharknado movies, Charles Hittinger also starred alongside Tara Reid in American Reunion. Horror fans might just remember Connor

Weil from the Scream TV series.

Opening scene: It gets right into the action briefly as we see some sharks in the water who are quickly dragged into the air by a tornado. The opening Sharknado title then gets 'blown away' and we are told the scene is 20 miles off the coast of Mexico. Two guys, one the captain of the ship they are on, are negotiating a price for shark fins. Lightening strikes though and the boat starts rocking - there's a storm brewing! The CGI is pretty bad as soon as we see the sharks. One guy working on the boat gets eaten by a shark that has unfortunately landed on the vessel. The captain and the guy buying the sharks have now had a disagreement and are shooting at each other on the deck. A shark eats the guy who was buying, but soon after the boat is taken by a tornado. Well, obviously a sharknado because as it rises we see the captain eaten by a shark.

Awfully Good character: John Heard plays George. He's the local at the bar that Fin runs and in lesser hands he's just the old drunk perv at the bar. He still is that a little bit to be honest but he's likeable and they give him enough back-story to make you feel something when he does eventually die. And if you weren't on board before, he does save a young girl and a dog shortly before he is eaten by a shark.

Awfully Good scene: Fin could have been the Awfully Good character above because he is such a ridiculous stereotypical American hero that it's pretty much a parody. Which leads us to this scene. While trying to escape the sharknado, the group lead by Fin come across a school bus. They can't see if there's anyone on it and don't want to risk getting close to it so, against everyone else's decision, Fin decides he has to save the kids inside (remember, he doesn't actually know if there's any kids inside). They drive on to a bridge above the school bus and luckily, Finn has some rope and rock climbing gear with him. With this equipment he abseils (they use the word rappel but it's the same thing) down from the bridge to land on top of the car. Thankfully (well, for Fin), there is a group of school children and a driver in the bus. He then has to attach them to a rope and have them pulled back up from above. We don't see this in real time because I assume it took several hours because there's at least twenty kids. I agree with Tara Reid who said it's not really worth the risk. Fin saves them all and just about survives as a shark starts leaping up at him as he makes his way up to safety.

Awfully Good line: There's some pretty bad dialogue in Sharknado. When one woman is surrounded by red water with a shark attacking her, one character says "Looks like it's that time of the month".
The bus driver sadly dies shortly after being saved. He tells the people around him that "My mum always told me Hollywood would kill me." Just as a letter from the Hollywood sign lands on him and flattens him.
There is actually one truly Awfully Good line though. The group are heading away from the sharknado in search of Fin's son. They drive past an old people's home and this exchange happens:
"Why's there a retirement home next to an airport?"
"Cos old people can't hear?"
Just on its own it's a funny because it's bad line but in the context of the movie it's odder/funnier. The retirement home plays no part in the movie. It absolutely does not need to be mentioned at all. There's no link. It's like the script writer had a joke he thought was funny and just had to fit it in the film some how.

Other notes and scenes: On a re-watch, I'd forgotten that the CGI in this first movie is really quite bad. Even compared to the other Sharknado movies. It's only ten years old but clearly the budget was not great. Fin is immediately the hero from the first scene he is in. He shouts shark a lot when he sees a friend get attacked by one but no-one on the packed beach listens to him. Eventually people see the water is turning red and Fin saves the day. Mostly. Some people still get eaten. Fin can't escape them though because shortly after, a shark lands in the bar and is stabbed by an oar. A giant Ferris wheel gets away from whatever is holding it up due to the waves and wind but doesn't just fall down. It starts rolling! We see one guy get squashed by it. Finn and his gang are driving through about three foot of water at one point when a shark starts swimming underneath their car. When Fin gets to his ex-wive's and daughters house to save them, they're not really that bothered. No-ones quite sure that this is a sharknado yet. The new boyfriend is taken out by a shark through the window and then people start realising things are serious. They manage to save the guys legs but nothing else. The house is immediately flooded though but when we see outside it's completely clear of rain water. It must have been their swimming pool that overflowed or something. As soon as they escape, the house completely collapses. The water damage was clearly quite severe. As they drive away a shark bites the roof open but then they suddenly with the head on the end (which is probably exactly what was happening). There's a fantastically cheesy couple of scenes involving the love story part of the film. At the start of the film, we hear about the power malfunction that is constantly causing problems with the caged area. No-one seems that bothered that this could cause the sabretooths to escape. Several of the death scenes are fun. There's more than one decapitation, intestines being eaten and a sabretooth blown up. All this with quite a bit of blood and gore. The reason the sabretooth keep eating and never seem to be full is because they are bulimic. Yes, really. Towards the end of the film we discover there is a giant mutant sabretooth that only has its front two legs working, so kind of drags itself along the ground. The CGI for this sabretooth isn't actually too bad and there was one moment when you could see it running towards a guy through his sunglasses, which was the coolest image in the film.

Final scene: The best was left until last. Throughout the film there is a golden statue of a sabretooth on top of the park's main building. It is a CGI statue with the worst CGI i think I've ever seen. It also seems to change in size at different points in the film. The final scenes shows the parks owner Niles, frantically running away from the sabretooth inside the building. He manages to escape to the outside but the statues tusk is knocked off from the banging of the actual sabretooth inside. Unfortunately for Niles he is standing just beneath as the tusk falls into his mouth and out the back of his neck in an awfully good moment with terrible CGI. It's spectacular and crappy all at the same time. Just after this, the film kind of ends all of a sudden with, I presume, a few of the characters surviving.

Final thoughts: Attack of the Sabretooth is a very typical Awfully Good film. It really is awful but there's alot of fun with the death scenes to the terrible CGI to the stereotypical characters. It really is awfully good.

BLUBBERELLA (2011)

'She will kick ass, with her big ass'

Synopsis: An action comedy centred on an overweight woman whose footsteps cause explosions and whose dual swords are used against anyone who makes fun of her.

Director: Uwe Boll has quite the reputation. Unfortunately for him, it's for making poorly received movies. I think BloodRayne was the first movie that got him some what noticed (he got Ben Kingsley in for that one.) He also directed Jason Statham's worst movie - In The Name of the King.

Cast: Lindsay Hollister plays Blubberella. She has appeared as a one-off in a few TV shows and consistently in the Breaking Bad rip-off, Breaking Fat. Brendan Fletcher will be known to horror fans for starring in Freddy vs Jason, Leprechaun Origins and the Ginger Snaps sequels. He usually puts in an entertaining performance as proved in last year's seasonal horror Violent Night. Michael Pare also appeared in the Awfully Good Komodo vs Cobra and many many other films, including Vampire Penance: The Atonement of John Wolf, The Wild Man: Skunk Ape and Puppet Master: The Littlest Reich. Clint Howard has had a long career. He voiced the elephant in The Jungle Book in 1967! He also managed to star in the same year, the classic, Apollo 13 and the Awfully Good Ice Cream Man. A year after Blubberella, William Belli came to prominence as a contestant on the fourth season of Ru Paul's Drag Race and has since gone on to be a YouTube star, release a book, several music albums and continue a career on screen.

Opening scene: It's not the exciting start I hoped for. It shows Blubberella half amusingly swinging swords about and then introduces us to her daily life, starting with the half vampire, half human making a very big breakfast.

Awfully Good character: It has to be Blubberella herself! Half human, half vampire. She is not quite Blade. Never moving at a pace quicker than slow jog she still manages to kill off plenty of Nazi's with her sword throwing and swinging skills. She's pretty good with a gun too. She's not as funny as she thinks she is but does have some interesting dreams, including befriending Hitler.

Awfully Good line: Most of the comedy lines were just awful, so this is the best it had. Blubberella's fighting is described as *"like a caged rhino that hasn't been fed in weeks."*. That's as good as it gets.

Awfully Good scene: I've already mentioned it briefly but Blubberella and Adolf Hitler (played by director Uwe Boll) becoming friends in one of her dreams was mildly amusing. We see clips of them playing games, chatting and giving each other advice.

Other notes and scenes: The music throughout is awful. It's supposed to be 'cheesy' but it's still rubbish. There's several scenes of Blubberella and her 'army' of friends fighting Nazi's but it's never as exciting as it should be. One of the funniest moments I didn't even understand. A guy dressed as a fish turns up in a few of the scenes, just in the background really. Not doing much of note but it's somehow funny. History isn't really paid attention to here. I guess the director thinks its funny to have a film set during World War II but having the characters using mobile phones and the internet. There's a whole scene copied from the film Precious. Most of the characters are awful stereotypes. Especially the gay character. There's also insults to him such as 'fag'. Oh, and there's even a black character who is a white guy painted black!!! If that's not enough to put you off this film I'm not sure what is. There's a lot of 'easy' humour. People hiding behind small branches they are holding, for instance. The characters even say things like "We are doing this because the scripts says we have to.". This is not a clever film.

Final scene: As expected there's some gun fighting between Blubberella and her men and the Nazi's. Plenty of cheap-looking CGI explosions and it all ends when Blubberella kills a guy by sitting on his face and farting. And if that wasn't enough, as the credits role we get treated to a preview of Blubberella at Christmas.

Final thoughts: Blubberella is not Awfully Good. It is just plain awful.

OCTOPUS (2000)

'There is no escape. Above, or below the water!'

Synopsis: An American nuclear submarine is transporting a captured terrorist to the States. The terrorist's henchmen, however, are planning to hijack the sub and rescue their leader. Meanwhile, a large, unidentified creature is approaching the sub at high speed.

Director: John Eyres slowly worked as a director from 1987 (Lucifer) until 2006's Irish Jam. If horror fans don't know him from Octopus, you might remember Ripper which starred Kelly Brook.

Cast: Jay Harrington's most notable roles are in S.W.A.T. the TV series, American (Pie) Reunion and in several episodes of Desperate Housewives. Ravil Isyanov has appeared in several well known titles in both film and TV. Including Eastenders, Buffy the Vampire Slayer, GLOW, Goldeneye and Transformers: Dark Side of the Moon. David Beecroft hasn't done any film or TV work since 2000 but did appear in Creepshow 2 (the excellent segment 'Hitch-hiker) early in his career. Carolyn Lowery has also seemingly retired from acting but does have some horror credentials after appearing in Candyman. Ricco Ross's horror C.V. includes Aliens and Wishmaster. Aswell as 2014 film Bermuda Tentacles, which looks almost identical to Octopus! Mariana Stansheva might not act so much now but she has been the casting director for films such as The Offering, The Princess, Jolt, and The Hitman's Wife's Bodyguard.

Opening scene: We rewind to 1962 and the Cuban missile crisis. A Russian submarine is about to be torpedoed by an American submarine. There's arguments inside the Russian one which leads to the captain shooting someone. These arguments are actually in Russian with subtitles, which I was surprised they bothered with. The torpedo hits and the submarine sinks. But most importantly we see the cargo of barrels that we on board, fall into the sea and leak what I assume was toxic waste. Toxic waste that might effect some creatures swimming nearby. Maybe.

Awfully Good Character: Casper played by Ravil Isyanov. The character obviously has a great name to start with. Casper is the villain of the film, even more so than the octopus actually. But unfortunately he is about as menacing as the ghost he shares a name with. He will feature alot in the rest of this write up. But he dresses up as an elderly woman, sets bombs, kills people and even gets on the wrong side of the octopus. He is played as a crazy, psychotic who is dangerous because he's so unpredictable but it doesn't quite work. Isyanov actually plays the role quite well and it probably would have worked better in a different film.

Awfully Good line: This line needs a bit of context. Casper, after faking a seizure and escaping his handcuffs in a room in the submarine, manages to grab a guy and hold a piece of glass to his throat. Roy (Harrington) is also there and trying to talk Casper out of it. The guy then says to Roy, *"Don't do it sir, I'm ready to die."* It's an hilarious line. There is no need for him to die, even if Casper gets out of the room, there's not a whole lot he can do to escape a submarine thousands of metres below the sea. Maybe the guy was secretly depressed and thought he might aswell die now.

Awfully Good scene: Casper features here again. I guess he was the star of this film.
He manages to actually escape the submarine and board a cruise liner along with a few other people. From here he actually manages to get a helicopter away, mainly because Roy seemingly can't shoot people, even if they've killed hundreds of people. When I say can't, I don't mean he attempts and misses, I mean he doesn't even pull the trigger. Anyway, Casper is on the helicopter, gloating about his escape. But it seems the octopus didn't like his cockiness. Because with one tentacle he swiftly kills Casper amazingly precisely. And then grabs the helicopter and brings that crashing down.

Other notes and scenes: Right at the start of the film, Casper is dressed as an old woman. It is very clear it is a man dressed as a woman but no-one including two CIA agents notice. But he does arouse suspicion when they notice a bag he had five minutes ago, he no longer has. This turns out to be a bomb and there's a massive explosion. People fly away from it in slow-motion and flames shoot from the building. This leads to Casper being chased by the two agents. One of whom is overweight and quite old. But he gives chase and manages to do alot better at keeping up than the younger more in shape agent. The overweight guy also has the funniest and slowest looking run I've ever seen. Unfortunately he dies not long after, from a bomb. Which, just as he realises is going to go off in his hands, he has the greatest 'ooooooh bollocks' expression on his face. We then hear that this is the ninth embassy Casper has bombed in two years. He did get caught here by the way and for someone so experienced is amazingly crap at his 'job'. The first sight of the octopus comes at over thirty minutes into the film, and we don't really see alot. There are alot of scenes when the submarine gets rocked by the octopus. Here, the camera moves from side to side and the actors move about like they are in an earthquake. Of course it looks awful (ly Good). The Russians on the cruise liner to save Casper, shoot a cleaner while she holds up a white duvet. It looked like a ghost had been killed. The octopus is pretty huge by the way, bigger than the submarine. For some reason it attacks the submarine even when it is grounded and stationary. I'm not really sure why. The only real female character spends a whole lot of time in just her underwear. The octopus eventually manages to get its tentacles into the submarine and grabs a few people away. I'm not sure how it could really see them though, just got lucky I guess. The CGI for the octopus isn't actually too bad, even in the last ten minutes when we see alot more of it.

Final scene: Not quite as dramatic as I hoped but Roy manages to be the hero, despite being a bit of a wimp. He drives an escape pod of sorts, with the bomb into the octopus's mouth. Managing to leap out of it just in time so he survived. The bomb had about three minutes left to go off when he received it, but somehow in the film, time seemed to slow down before he used it. It should have gone off earlier. Everyone celebrates as the credits start to roll.

Final thoughts: Octopus might have been more fun to review than it was to watch. Although it is Awfully Good, you will be laughing throughout a lot of the film at how bad it is. I guess that's sometimes the point?

ATTACK OF THE SABRETOOTH (2005)

'Extinct no more'

Synopsis: In the Fiji islands, the greedy and unscrupulous owner of the Valalola Resort Primal Park invites investors and guests for an opening party of his compound composed of a hotel and zoo aiming to find partners for his discoveries. When a bunch of college small-time thieves puts a virus in the security system to participate in a scavenger hunt, the greatest attractions of the zoo - sabretoothes from the prehistoric age developed from DNA found in fossils - escape.

Director: Attack of the Sabre Tooth was the last film of George Miller's career. He's most notable film is probably The Never Ending Story II: The Next Chapter, which I, like many others I'm sure, have not seen.

Cast: Robert Carridine has been in films as varied as Django Unchained and Lizzie McGuire. But also the likes of Jurassic Wars: Sharktopus vs Pteracuda and Slumber Party Slaughter. Cleopatra Coleman was in the Australian soap opera Neighbours and has recently appeared in the show Dopesick and Brandon Cronenberg movie Infinity Pool. Nicholas Bell was an accountant in Mission Impossible II and Zordan in Mighty Morphin Power Rangers: The Movie. Stacy Haiduk has been in many TV shows including Superboy, Melrose Place, Heroes, Prison Break and True Blood. Billy Aaron Brown I recognised as Kyle from 8 Simple Rules. While Parry Shen appeared in Hatchet I, II and III and Bonnie Piesse played Beru Lars in both Star Wars Episode II and III. Brian Wimmer hasn't starred in any film or show since 2013 but he featured in A Nightmare On elm Street Part 2: Freddy's Revenge and Tank Girl.

Opening scene: A security guy takes a break to read (well, maybe just look at) a porn magazine. He is interrupted on the walkie talkie when his favourite page of the magazine flies into a caged area of the island. I assume the guy knew a sabretooth was in the caged area but he wondered in anyway, and even left the gate wide open. We then see through the sabretooth's eyes, in a Predator-style heat map moment. The sabretooth attacks, ripping the guys arm off, with some pretty good looking blood and gore. We then see close-ups of the sabretooth's face as he kills the guy.

Awfully Good character: As usual with Awfully Good films this is chock-a-block with stereotypes. The group of teenagers being the most obvious here, the 'jock', the 'princess', the Asian tech genius and maybe worst of all, the 'goth'. But my favourite was Grant, the cigar smoking arrogant millionaire who is generally just pretty annoying and eventually gets his head bitten off.

Awfully Good line: There was only really two to pick from. And I'm going to go for one from Grant. When talking about the parks owner he says *"If his brains were dynamite, he couldn't even blow his nose"*. This film didn't have the cleverest of scripts.

Awfully Good scene: It was probably the final scene but that will be spoke about later. Apart from that, there was a great moment when one character's head is swiftly bitten off by the sabretooth but in the moments after, the rest of the body comically keeps walking, minus a head, before it collapses to the floor, blood spurting everywhere.

Other notes and scenes: Early on in the film there's a sex scene seen from a CCTV camera. Well I say seen, but we get to see naked legs and feet moving about next to a pile of clothes. But the security guy watching it was happy enough. Speaking of the CCTV, the ones used in this film are awful. In the scenes it's shown, we can see it shows a close up of a fence which is no help to anyone, and I never once saw any animal on it.
After the opening scene, the gate is still open. One person goes to see what has happened and obviously walks in the caged area, leaving the gate open again. When he is then killed off, another security guard sees what is going on. Of course he leaves the gate open and once again is killed. No-one then bothers looking for the three guys or closes the gate.
Instead of CGI occasionally, a model head is used for the sabretooths. Normally I'd love the use of a model but it looks awful and when it moves through the grass, the way it moves looks like some guy is holding a stick

with the head on the end (which is probably exactly what was happening). There's a fantastically cheesy couple of scenes involving the love story part of the film. At the start of the film, we hear about the power malfunction that is constantly causing problems with the caged area. No-one seems that bothered that this could cause the sabretooths to escape. Several of the death scenes are fun. There's more than one decapitation, intestines being eaten and a sabretooth blown up. All this with quite a bit of blood and gore. The reason the sabretooth keep eating and never seem to be full is because they are bulimic. Yes, really. Towards the end of the film we discover there is a giant mutant sabretooth that only has its front two legs working, so kind of drags itself along the ground. The CGI for this sabretooth isn't actually too bad and there was one moment when you could see it running towards a guy through his sunglasses, which was the coolest image in the film.

Final scene: The best was left until last. Throughout the film there is a golden statue of a sabretooth on top of the park's main building. It is a CGI statue with the worst CGI i think I've ever seen. It also seems to change in size at different points in the film. The final scenes shows the parks owner Niles, frantically running away from the sabretooth inside the building. He manages to escape to the outside but the statues tusk is knocked off from the banging of the actual sabretooth inside. Unfortunately for Niles he is standing just beneath as the tusk falls into his mouth and out the back of his neck in an awfully good moment with terrible CGI. It's spectacular and crappy all at the same time. Just after this, the film kind of ends all of a sudden with, I presume, a few of the characters surviving.

Final thoughts: Attack of the Sabretooth is a very typical Awfully Good film. It really is awful but there's alot of fun with the death scenes to the terrible CGI to the stereotypical characters. It really is awfully good.

SEATTLE SUPERSTORM (2012)

'A disaster of epic proportions'

Synopsis: When an unidentified object is shot down by the military and crashes into Puget Sound, it sets off a series of strange weather phenomena: earthquakes, tornadoes, lightning storms.

Director: Jason Bourque. Director of the previously mentioned Stonados.

Cast: Esai Morales has a lot of films and shows to his name including From Dusk Til Dawn (TV), Doomsday Man, Jericho, How To Get Away With Murder and the upcoming Master Gardener. Ona Grauer starred in Elysium and also appeared in the films based on video games, Alone in the Dark and House of the Dead. She has only starred in one film since the under-seen Come To Daddy. MacKenzie Porter has appeared in episodes of the children's horror show R.L. Stine's Haunting Hour, aswell as an episode of Supernatural but is perhaps better known for her music. Jesse Moss has a decent horror C.V. including Tucker and Dale vs Evil, Final Destination 2, Ginger Snaps, Still/Born and The Uninvited. Martin Cummins starred in Friday the 13th Part VIII: Jason Takes Manhattan and the TV series Poltergeist: The Legacy. More recently he played Mayor Keller in Riverdale. Michelle Harrison starred in the TV series The Flash as Nora Allen and appeared in the excellent sci-fi/horror Freaks. Jay Brazeau has 278 credits on IMDb! Including Watchmen, Insomnia and two episodes of The X-Files. Still going strong, he starred in Antlers in 2021 and the Day of the Dead series in the same year. Matty Finochio also showed up in Day of the Dead and appeared in Riverdale and The Chilling Adventures of Sabrina. Jared Abrahamson played CPL Cole in Fear of the Walking Dead.

Opening scene: This is kept short and sweet but dramatic. There's some sort of an electrical storm in a city. I assume Seattle. We can see a big tower and people are running around frantically in the wind. The camera pans to a tornado nearby, as a character looks towards it. The screen then goes to black and we are told we are going back nine hours earlier.

Awfully Good character: Jacob Stinson. He's a Lieutenant, I think. But he just seems to be trying his hardest to be the reason a lot of people will be killed. He of course, wants no outside interference from any government or anyone on stopping the storm. Any expert advice he'll ignore. Especially if it means trying to save peoples lives. Thankfully he is also involved in my favourite scene that will be mentioned later. He has some pretty funny lines too, including, when answering "You cannot wipe out Seattle!" he says "It's my city, my decision!".

Awfully Good line: Our heroes get a message from the president just before they're about to save the world. Well, save Seattle. We don't see the president say this, the main character just claims she has the message to pass on. **"The difference between success and failure is thinking the impossible is possible".** Inspirational stuff.

Awfully Good scene: Jacob Stinson's death scene. In a heated argument with the lead female, Emma, she tells the nearby army officers (I think that's who they are) to arrest Jacob. But they have no idea who to take orders from. Despite this, Jacob makes a run for it only to be hit with a lightening bolt! Destroying him in one quick flash.

Other notes and scenes: Several things happen quite a lot in Seattle Superstorm. Bad CGI, explosions, people running about in the wind and some army folk seating infront of computer screens panicking a little. Half a human skull is found at the site of a storm but for some reason the experts think it's an alien skull. Turns out I was right though, it was human. There's the odd earthquake scene, which consists of the camera shaking all over the place while people hold on to anything they can. In a pretty cool moment, some guy whose hand is mummified (he touched something he shouldn't have), suddenly has his hand crumble away. The giant tower is shown a lot in all its Awfully Good glory. The storm around it then hits it and it collapses to the ground causing two of our main characters to crash their car. Unfortunately, it's not raining, because 'heavy' water is
needed to put a stop to it all. This is kind of explained but not very well and it's all overly complicated. One of my favourite moments involved

Russian bio-chemist Dimitri Kandinsky, sacrificing himself to save the city. He goes underground to turn on a manual valve for some water. I have no idea why he couldn't just go back up the ladder when he'd done it but apparently this couldn't happen and he had to die. The tornado we see is via some Awfully Good CGI. It manages to destroy a helicopter which went to take some water somewhere. I wasn't sure using a helicopter was the best plan of action.

Final scene: The family have put all their differences aside and plan on saving the city. They drive around to the main area of the storm as some sort of tentacles start growing from the ground to the sky. This is due to some weird chemical reaction but really looks like some Jack and the Beanstalk-type situation. From the trucks, our main characters use hoses to spray the tentacles. It takes a surprisingly little amount of water to stop them growing and make them disappear and thus, ending the superstorm. The sun appears for the first time and everyone goes home happy with a wedding to plan.

Final thoughts: Weather based Awfully Good films aren't quite as exciting as creature based ones. Seattle Superstorm does all the usual things a film like this does. It's quite dramatic, and at times fun, but nothing special if you've seen more than a couple of these films before.

MALIBU SHARK ATTACK (AKA MEGA SHARK IN MALIBU) (2009)

'The tsunami was just the beginning of the terror'

Synopsis: A tsunami floods Malibu and unleashes a hunting pack of deep-water prehistoric goblin sharks, targeting a group of lifeguards trapped in their half-submerged station on stilts and a team of construction workers stranded in a flooded house.

Director: David Lister was previously in charge of The Last Leprechaun, The Meeksville Ghost and Kwagga Strikes Back. He's only directed two movies since 2009 including a 'dark twist' on Beauty and the Beast.

Cast: Remi Broadway has had very small parts in The Marine and Scooby-Doo. Warren Christie has mainly featured in TV work including The Exorcist, Chicago Fire and Batwoman (as Bruce Wayne) but also starred in space-based horror Apollo 18 and the McG directed This Means War. Mungo McKay has appeared in Undead, Bullets for the Dead and Daybreakers. Evert McQueen appeared in the very good The Horseman, The Condemned and a couple of episodes of the British show Heartbeat. Sonya Salomaa has a few horrors to her name including House of the Dead and Hollow Man 2. Peta Wilson has starred in The League of Extraordinary Gentleman and Superman Returns. Finally, Chelan Simmons is a bit of a scream queen. Her first movie (TV) appearance was in Stephen King's It and since then she has starred in Final Destination 3, Tucker and Dale vs Evil, See No Evil 2, Wind Chill and the TV show Hannibal.

Opening scene: Surprisingly very short and uneventful. There's an explosion underwater and some dangerous looking sharks appear shortly after as the opening credits role.

Awfully Good character: Jenny played by the scream queen herself, Chelan Simmons. She plays the ditsy blonde teenager who is on community service for stealing stuff from a department store. She complains a little bit about this but seems to mostly enjoy walking about in a bikini. Jenny overreacts to pretty much everything and does a lot of screaming. The scene in which she has her leg stitched up actually has some pretty good practical effects. But like all Awfully Good films, her character does fall in love with one of the films heroes.

Awfully Good line: And Jenny gets this award to. When she is asked how she's feeling after cutting her leg and then having it stitched up, she replies with *"Like I stuck it in a blender!"*. Sounds very painful!

Awfully Good scene: This one was built up in a way that you knew exactly what was going to happen. One of the several love stories is built up for most of the first half of the film and one couple are now engaged. They have a very small disagreement before announcing their love for each other just in time for a shark to leap through the floor of the flooded beach hut and grab the girl with its teeth. The water turns red as she disappears. But the end of the scene brings the highlight as the guy who has just lost his fiancée is hilariously devastated by the incident. Whaling, while the other characters stop him from, I assume, jumping in and getting revenge. I almost felt bad for laughing at him.

Other notes and scenes: There is one shot of a shark opening its mouth wide as it swims closer to the camera, seemingly to eat someone, that is used at least five times. The exact same CGI shot over and over again. Malibu Shark Attack fits in four love stories too! The newly engaged couple, the girl who has an ex and new boyfriend both nearby, the teen trying to get with the lifeguard and another couple who last a matter of minutes. The CGI is of course Awfully Good, mainly for the sharks but the waves were poorly done too. When the tsunami hits, a few people decide that as the highway is jammed, it's best to head back to the beach. I guess as they didn't die immediately so it was the right idea somehow. The tsunami produced one hundred foot waves apparently but the hut that everyone survived in, was about 20 foot high. It somehow survived in quite good shape and did not fill with water much. The facial expressions from the main characters in anticipation of the wave hitting might be the highlight of the film. In fairness to the actors, the expressions are probably quite normal for this situation but the camera stays on close-ups of there faces for way too long and we just look at shocked and scared faces for about a minute. Of course, we have one shark leap out of the water to kill one character and of course there's one character who wants to trap and not kill the sharks because they have a use for science. They always do. Towards the end of the film, the boat they hope to escape with runs out of fuel and they decide they need to drift to shore. This obviously took a while because from bright sunshine, the next scene is set in darkness. The dark, flooded building is actually the most horror-like part of the film.

Final scene: It's a bit of a let down. Our survivors have one shark to kill. In the flooded building they manage to trap it very quickly and they all stab, hit or buzz-saw it to its death with a little bit of blood splatter to boot. Everything is wrapped up then with a news report and a helicopter rescue. But there is one more oddity to end the film. Unfortunately for one woman, her ex and her current boyfriend survived and are still arguing over her. To which she suggests they should just 'share' her! She quickly changes her mind and decides a coin toss would work things out.

Final thoughts: I enjoyed Malibu Shark Attack but I'm not entirely sure why. It definitely doesn't take itself seriously, it's over the top and generally fun. For reasons unknown to myself I've seen it at least three times

BATS (1999)

*'Where do you hide when
the dark is alive?'*

Synopsis: Bats, the result of a government experiment gone wrong, have suddenly become intelligent, vicious, and omnivorous, and are attacking people near Gallup, Texas. Bat specialist Sheila Casper and her assistant Jimmy are brought in but can they stop the bats before the military comes in and, in their ignorance, makes things worse?

Director: Louis Morneau seems to like sequels. His films include Carnosaur 2, The Hitcher 2: I've Been Waiting and Joy Ride 2: Dead Ahead. His last film, Werewolf: The Beast Among Us was released in 2012.

Cast: Lou Diamond Philips has worked a lot but not many films with a title as good as Metal Tornado. Dina Meyer is of course best known for the fantastic Starship Troopers and Johnny Mnemonic but horror fans will also recognise her from Saw. She also appeared in one episode of American Horror Story Apocalypse. Some of Bob Gunton's many credits include Shawshank Redemption, Argo, The Lincoln Lawyer, the Daredevil Netflix show and Ghostbusters: Afterlife. Leon (just the one name) is best known for his lead role in Cool Runnings. He recently showed up in the series Swarm. Carlos Jacott has appeared in many TV shows including Firefly, Ally McBeal and Frasier but also in some pretty popular movies such as Grosse Pointe Blank and Being John Malkovich. Ned Bellamy also appeared in Saw and Shawshank Redemption, aswell as Django Unchained, Twilight, Wind Chill and Mystery Men. James Sie works mostly as a voice actor. He has the distinction of voicing Jackie Chan in the show Jackie Chan Adventures but has also produced voice work in Kung-Fu Panda, Star Trek: Lower Decks and many video games including the Final Fantasy VII Remake and Ghosts of Tsushima.

Opening scene: We're in Gallup, Texas. A couple are in a car, I'm sure they're about to make out when a bat flies past. Then a bat smashes through the window and attacks them. We don't see a lot as the image flashes every half a second. The guy is eventually somehow thrown through the windscreen. By a bat I assume.

Awfully Good character: Bob Gunton as mad scientist Dr. Alexander McCabe. He begins as a slightly evil scientist, as he was the one that made these bats evil and human eating, as well as intelligent. By the end we realise he enjoys doing it and wants to see them kill everyone. Gunton isn't overly convincing in the role but that's partly because it's almost too comedic for a film that is trying to be serious. Like all good mad scientists, he meets his demise when what he has created kills him as he steps outside and tells the bats "come to me". They oblige and eat him.

Awfully Good line: A few lines with the same theme.
"Guano?" "It's bat shit." "Trust me Sheriff, you don't want to die choking on no bat shit fumes." I don't think that's a way anybody would like to go.

Awfully Good scene: Dr. Tobe Hodge's death scene is Awfully Good in the cheesiest way. The character does much of nothing until he sees Dr. Sheila Casper (Meyer) dying at the hands of the bats. He distracts them, only for them to attack and kill him. Just at that moment the camera zooms in on Sheila with her hand reaching out as she cries "NOOOOOOOOO!". She is later sobbing saying "He saved me!". He died a hero. Even if he was boring for the rest of his life.

Other notes and scenes: Before the bats are blamed for the first killings, a kids satanic cult is thought to be at fault. Obviously, because why wouldn't they? But, it is of course a government scientific experiment gone wrong. It always is! The first attempt to capture the bats gives us a 1980's style montage video of the characters preparing their capture tools. Mainly just some big nets. Unsurprisingly there's a lot of people running away from bats. The CGI and practical effects actually aren't too bad. One of the few comedy moments happens when a bat flies into a car windscreen and bounces off like it had hit a brick wall without realising. But, the hundreds of bats then completely cover the car. They somehow manage to get in but at first a car cigarette lighter keeps a few at bay. Not for long as another bat is flying about inside the car. The sheriff decides the gun is the best solution, which doesn't seem like a good idea but it works. At one point we see a creepy bat sitting at the bottom of a babies cot while the unsuspecting baby sleeps. But that is it for that scene, nothing happens. I'm not suggesting I wanted to see the bat attack the baby but at least let me see someone save it! At some point the bats seem to get a lot bigger, you could almost call them giant bats. And with this they make a dinosaur-like noise. There's no explanation for this. None of the towns residents listen to the mayor when she warns them of killer bats (I'm not sure I would) but they regret this when the bats come flying down the main street. One police officer shouts "Get back!" at the bats while pointing a gun. I'm not sure if he thought it would work but there was a bat on his back anyway (this and the line may have been a Awfully Good joke) and it kills him quite violently. A car also explodes in the main street mayhem. I'm not sure how but it looked dramatic. Country music plays aloud during a lot of this conflict and then the guns are bought out. Some people aimlessly shooting in the air, while some, such as the main police officer, have ridiculously good aim. He just picks off flying bats one shot at a time. The characters then discover that the government plan on bombing the area in 48 hours if they don't sort it out. Even though this probably wont kill the bats. So they take cover in a school and we get a new eighties-style montage when they board up the school to protect them for the night. That night the school attack involves a flame thrower, bat vision, a bat attached to the end of the camera and random close-ups of stuffed animals. But our main characters survive. Which is more than can be said for the army, who tried to eliminate the bats but all end up dead.

Final scene: Our two heroes decide to go to the mine where the bats are living and freeze them dead. They put on a couple of space suits and go on their mission. Just the one bat attacks them at first but it's burnt with a flare. They eventually manage to turn some kind of freezer on and are then chased out by the bats. Lots of electrical explosions make things a bit more exciting and the entrances are blown up and sealed at the same time just as the two characters escape. Like so many Awfully Good movies I was sure one or two bats would survive. And Bats teases this with one little bat survivor, but it's then quickly run over.

Final thoughts: Bats suffers from taking itself way too seriously. If they'd gone with a bit more comedy and used the mad scientist character more, this could have been more enjoyable. It's still very watchable but should have been more entertaining.

PEGASUS VS. CHIMERA (2011)

'Two legendary creatures. A battle for the ages'

Synopsis: A father hunts with his son, slays a monstrous dragon and is confronted by a corrupt tyrant who forces them into battle.

Director: John Bradshaw, not the wrestler, has directed a lot of TV movies, lots of Christmas based ones - The Christmas Cure, Santa's Squad and Best Christmas Party ever included. He now seems to be settled into TV movie rom-coms and his last films seem to have basically the same cover artwork with a man and woman standing next to each other. These include, Love in Whitbrooke, How To Find Forever and Lucless In Love. Pegasus Vs Chimera sticks out like a sore thumb in his directed films.

Cast: Sebastian Roche looks a bit like Gordon Ramsey. He's been in a whole lot of stuff including 2013 werewolf film Wer and an episode of Guillermo del Toro's Cabinet of Curiosities. Nazneen Contractor has a strange surname and has appeared in 21 episodes of 24 and Star Trek Into Darkness. More recently she voiced Synara San in Star Wars: Resistance and showed up in Spiral: From the Book of Saw. Rae Dawn Chong appeared in the Arnie film Commando and has had a recent resurgence starring in the shows American Crime Story and Interview With The Vampire. Tig Fong mainly works as a stunt guy and has worked on stunts for the shows What We Do In The Shadows and The Boys and films such as X-Men: Dark Phoenix, It and many more. He's acted plenty of times too, including What We Do In the Shadows again, Hemlock Grove, Lost Girl and Assault On Precinct 13. Carlo Rota also appeared in 24 and Saw V. Aswell as more recently in an episode of Agents of S.H.E.I.L.D. Jason Gosbee is another stunt guy turned actor who has done stunt work for The Boys, Locke and

Key, Firestarter, and Clarice, to name but a few. And there's yet another stunt worker with Bernadette Couture who has worked on Mayor of Kingstown, Becky and Shazam!

Opening scene: A father and son are out hunting a dinosaur. As you do. The son is a bit useless and just as the dinosaur is about to kill him, his father saves him and kills the dinosaur with his sword. There's an annoying shaky camera throughout this scene. Soon after, two guys come and claim they are trespassing on the emperors land, a fight ensures. And as the son runs away he sees his father stabbed with a sword and promises to avenge his death.

Awfully Good character: King Orthos played by Carlo Rota is the Awfully Good villain of the film. He's never really that menacing. Him and his 'army' all seem to be skinheads. Like a Eastender's Mitchell army. He occasionally comes to life with his sword and seems slightly threatening.

Awfully Good line: *"I can rain down a storm of arrows like you have never seen."* A somewhat threat by Princess Philony.

Awfully Good scene: Just for its ridiculousness, I'm going with the Chimera's entrance. The villains do some kind of ritual and the chimera comes out of his King Orthos' mouth. Not just in its present form but in some kind of smoke that forms its body. We then learn that it can search for souls at the villains command.

Other notes and scenes: There are a few gruesome scenes even if we don't see a lot. Such as a guy getting decapitated while his daughter watches (I think someone had been watching Game of Thrones!). The witch of the film knows literally everything. She has visions you see, which tell her details about every character, their history and future. She is the one that summons the Pegasus, from the stars. She then makes its reins just appear in her hands from nowhere. The Pegasus is always in disguise by the way. So we only see its wings when it's in the air. It's just a horse when grounded. And of course, the world will end if the Pegasus dies or is not returned to the stars by midnight. It almost feels like it wasn't worth summoning it. The CGI for the flying Pegasus is not great. It's the least intimidating 'monster' I have seen to date. Oh, one final thing, the Pegasus can heal who ever rides it. Even from near death. The princess of the film seems to be wearing Lycra trousers. I'm not sure what fantasy era this is supposed to be in but no-one else is wearing anything that stylish. The witch dies seconds after telling the Chimera "foolish beast, you can't penetrate the power of the pentagon!". The sword fights are all pretty average but the big main fight at least takes place in a waterfall! When the Chimera attacks some people the CGI means it looks like it barely touches them. They still go flying through the air and get injured badly though.

Final scene: It comes down to the princess Vs. the emperor and of course the Chimera vs the Pegasus! The emperor is soon killed with a sword and the Pegasus starts doing some damage. The Chimera just does a whole lot of running and ramming or head-butting the Pegasus. Despite what looks like some good boxing skills from the Pegasus (with its hoofs of course), it takes, the princess with her crossbow, the other guy with his sword and the Pegasus, to kill off the Chimera. The sword is thrown beautifully accurately at the Chimera and the Pegasus finally tramples it to death! They look up to the sky, that has more stars than sky and the Pegasus flies back to the moon (I think) before midnight and thus, saving the world!

Final thoughts: Pegasus Vs. Chimera takes itself way too seriously for a film with that title! But its absurdity and ridiculousness makes it a whole lot of fun. If you like Awfully Good films, there's no way you can't enjoy this!

SNAKES ON A TRAIN (2006)

'First planes... now trains!'

Synopsis: A Zombie curse is placed upon a woman, which causes her to have living snakes inside her. Brujo, who is looking after her, attempts to take her to Los Angeles on the train. After several confrontations on the train, Brujo's collection of snakes manage to separate themselves from their owner and go on the hunt.

Director: The most interesting thing about the director seems to be that for this film he is known as The Mallachi Brothers. Really, he is just Peter Mervis.

Cast: A.J. Castro has had small appearances in Dexter, NCIS and in WWE video games he has voiced John Cena, Alberto Del Rio and The Miz (who knew the wrestlers weren't just used to voice themselves?!)! Giovanni Bejarano starred in 666: The Beast and one episode of many TV shows including Two Broke Girls, Lucifer, The Rookie and The Big Bang Theory. Amelia Jackson-Gray has starred in the horror films Halloween Night and Zombie Hunters. Just a year after Snakes on a Train, Shannon Gayle Hurd appeared in Number 23 but hasn't starred in much else. Stephen A.F. Day appeared in House on the Hill and strangely has starred in one thing in the last 11 years, he played Davis David (stupid name) in Pretty Little Liars in 2017. Lola Folsberg seemingly only acted between the ages of 1 and 11 but managed to star in Mega Piranha, Torture Room, Halloween Night, Night of the Dead: Leben Tod and Alien Abduction!

Opening scene: During the opening credits a guy is carrying a woman to the Mexican/American border. They speak to each other in a language that wasn't English, the guy smokes something from a pipe and blows the smoke in the girls face. We see some snakes in some jars and the woman drinks something that makes her throw up some green goo. Following the goo is a snake! She continues to throw up more snakes when an American guy discovers the couple. Unfortunately for him, a snake bites and kills him.

Awfully Good character: Snakes on a Train isn't full of fun characters. But the ex-police officer wannabe cowboy was my favourite of a bad bunch. He claimed to be a police officer and used this to get a girl naked and make out with him. He is stopped by an actual police officer before it goes any further. He then shoots him and grazes his cheek. Why the guy didn't shoot the cowboy in the head or heart when he wanted to kill him I'm not sure. Shortly after he finds a gun from somewhere, I say finds because I assume if he had it earlier he would have used it.

Awfully Good line: The rather horrible, *"Your mothers cunt smells like carpet cleaner"*. Since looking this quote up I've discovered it's a copy of a quote from 1987 Mickey Rourke film Barfly.

Awfully Good scene: The ending was my favourite scene and I'll be mentioning that in a bit so I won't write too much. But it involved a giant snake eating the whole train! The size of the snake kind of comes out of nowhere but it at least livened things up.

Other notes and scenes: The main guy has some magic dust that he blows into peoples eyes. Thinking about it now, it just seems to temporarily blind them, so it might just be dust. The black and green goo that is thrown up has some magical power aswell but I was never sure exactly what the power was. The one big fight scene involved this guy and a big bald guy who picked him up a lot but never threw him anywhere. He is eventually stabbed in the throat by some strange knife and then kicked off of a moving train. There's actually some pretty impressive visual/make-up effects when a snake slides into somebodies wrist, is cut out, and then slides back into somebody else's wrist. It's bloody and quite gross looking. Another bloody scene involves a body part (I wasn't sure what exactly) being pulled out of the body through the skin. A few snakes then crawl out too. He somehow remains alive through all of that. From here there seems to be lots of snakes being thrown up by people. There's one great moment when a guy seems to be smoking a light bulb?! Is this a thing?? I have no idea. A normal sized snake is then crawling around the ticket collector.

In the next shot, it has somehow suddenly grown in size considerably and bites him to death. I have to give the film-makers some praise for the majority of the time using real snakes and only the odd bit of CGI (until the end). The lead guy is absolutely fearless when it comes to snakes! Perhaps the most shocking scene was a child being eaten by a big snake from the legs upwards. It's not even a very short scene as the terrified little girl screams in pain. Oh, and finally we discover that a blanket is all that is needed to get away from the snakes. Just cover them up and jump over.

Final scene: A guy is batting snakes off brilliantly with a serving tray. With that, and the blanket, I was sure they would be safe. The initial girl that was throwing up the goo then turns into a snake. Or vampire, it's hard to tell at first. But she quickly starts eating other snakes. This then escalates to her eating her boyfriend and turning into a giant snake. And when I say giant, I mean bigger than the train! It first manages to stop the train and then begins to eat it. I'm not really sure how the people inside knew this was happening but it didn't matter because none of them seem that shocked about the situation. That said, they jump out of the end of the train before the snake eats them all. Luckily, one guy has kept some magical necklace that he uses to create a magical spell. This spell is pretty great because it summons a tornado that sweeps the snake away to, well away from them. That whole moment is exactly as ridiculous and Awfully Good as it sounds. Finally, some of the passengers start walking to L.A., I guess they have no choice. And the camera focuses on a girls leg with a snake bite.

Final thoughts: There's a good movie in this idea somewhere. The creators of it at least put some effort into it with the visual effects. But really, it goes along pretty slowly with not a lot happening for way too long. The near perfect Awfully Good ending cannot save a bad film for the most part.

PRIMAL SPECIES (AKA CARNOSAUR 3: PRIMAL SPECIES) (1996)

'Terror will never be extinct!'

Synopsis: International terrorists get a surprise when their cargo turns out to contain living dinosaurs. The army commando team now have to think fast if they want to prevent the extinction of the human species, instead of the reptiles.

Director: In 2014 director Jonathan Winfrey directed the interestingly titled Christmas Icetastrophe. He's also directed Excessive Force 2: Force on Force and Blood Sport VII: Manhunt.

Cast: Actor Scott Valentine has appeared in To Sleep With A Vampire and My Demon Love. I see a link there. He also starred in a franchise that spans a TV series and two films but I have never heard of - Black Scorpion (Returns and Sting of the...). Rick Dean also starred in Carnosaur 2, as well as Blood Fist III. Anthony Peck sadly died aged 49 in 1996 but had a fewer bigger titles to his name, including Die Hard: With A Vengeance and In The Line Of Fire. Rodger Halston appeared in an episode of the True Detective TV series and before Primal Species, Alien Terminator! Terri J. Vaughn appeared in this crazily titled film - Don't Be A Menace To South Central While Drinking Your Juice In The Hood but more importantly starred in the movie I assume that one is spoofing - Friday. Stephen Lee is another actor who died too young. You'll recognise him from several things including TV shows Nip/Tuck, Bones and Dark Angel. Justina Vail has starred in The X-Files and Jerry Maguire. Cyril O'Reilly appeared in some great comedies including Airplane and Porky's. After a fifteen year absence from the screen, he came back for 2022's Pig killer. Michael

McDonald has gone on to star in many films. The Heat, Spy, Halloween Kills and three Austin Powers movies. Rodman Flender might be the most surprising appearance here. If you don't know the name, he hasn't acted in very much but he has directed some great stuff. These include Idle Hands, the excellent zombie movie Eat Brains Love and episodes of The Office and Scream. Oh, and Roger Corman produced this film.

Opening scene: We jump straight into the action as the army are driving down some roads when they are suddenly attacked by some terrorists who look like ninjas holding guns. There's a big gun fight, lots of explosions and many trucks being blown up. There's even a bazooka and of course lots of dramatic, slow motion moments of people getting killed. A lot of people die and its a fun few minutes.

Awfully Good character: He was hardly in the film but I wish the leader of the gun-holding ninjas featured much more. He didn't do much except barking out orders to the ninjas while looking cool in sunglasses.

Awfully Good line: *"I should have read my horoscope. Probably would have said avoid tight spaces and prehistoric creatures"* A quite funny line in a film that doesn't have many of them.

Awfully Good scene: This comes when the group believe they have killed one of the Carnosaurs. They have it laying on an operating table while the 'expert' takes a look at it. She soon explains that it is alive and healing very quickly from its wounds, comparing it to a lizard growing back its tail but much quicker. Personally, I would have started worrying then and maybe tried to have tied down or just killed the dinosaur. They do neither, then act surprised when it leaps from the table and attacks! It kills off one character and manages to escape.

Other notes and scenes: There's a few more scenes of the terrorists versus the army with lots of deaths. There's actually quite a lot of blood throughout the movie. The acting is perfectly Awfully Good from start to finish. There's a couple of strange camera movements during the film. My favourite being a sudden extreme zoom away from one characters face, complete with zoom sound effects. The dinosaurs themselves look okay. Well, what I mean to say is that my opinion kept changing during the film. It may be the camera movement or the angles but they go from looking awful, to quite good, to kind of comical. I like that it's not CGI and its just models but sometimes it was very obvious that was the case. Usually when they moved. The camera normally only stays on the dinosaurs for a second at a time, creating seizure-inducing scenes. Some Marines are called at one point for back-up. Only no-one tells the army, so when they suddenly appear they nearly shoot each other. There's some dramatic speeches by the army and some A-Team-like music. Oh, and of course the Carnosaurs are wanted alive for medical research reasons. These creatures/monsters/animals always are by someone. The highlight of the dinosaurs attacking is when they go for the head. Including one that gets completely ripped off!

Final scene: There's dinosaurs on the loose, guns shooting, blood everywhere and two survivors trying to escape the boat everything is on. Luckily for them, the two have some C4 and they manage to get some in a Carnosaurs mouth and blow his head off! But some more explosives are set and they need to get off the boat! Cue a timer and some running as they leap off the boat just as it explodes while fireworks go off! The two characters float in the water as the explosions happen. But! We go back on land and discover one dino has survived!

Final thoughts: Primal Species is okay but took itself too seriously for me. There's some good action, explosions and plenty of blood but nothing new to see. Although dinosaurs are a bit underused in the Awfully Good genre.

SHARKNADO 2: THE SECOND ONE (2014)

'Shark happens'

Synopsis: Fin and April are on their way to New York City, until a category seven hurricane spawns heavy rain, storm surges, and deadly Sharknadoes.

Director: Anthony C. Ferante. He obviously directed the very first Sharknado and all of its sequels. Before that he made a few low budget horror movies based on classic tales such as Headless Horseman and Hansel and Gretel. After the sixth Sharknado movie he took on the sea in Zombie Tidal Wave but since then he's stayed clear of horror and his last film was Crown Prince of Christmas.

Cast: Tara Reid returns for the sequel. Sharknado got her back in the limelight but the late nineties/early noughties were great for her, with roles in American Pie (and the sequels), Urban Legend, Cruel Intentions, Van Wilder and Josie and the Pussycats. American Reunion helped her get back on track but since Sharknado it's been a mixed bag of low budget genre films, with Party Bus To Hell and Charlie's Farm being the highlights. Ian Ziering was best known for Beverly Hills 90210 before he managed to get the lead Sharknado role. Since the Sharknado films he has had a decent role in the Swamp Thing show and popped up in the aforementioned Zombie Tidal Wave. He even got to play Finn in Lavantula . Vivica A. Fox of Kill Bill Vol. 1 & 2, Independence Day and Batman & Robin, shows up and doesn't do a whole lot. She seems to still act in at least half a dozen films a year. While Mark McGrath, lead singer of Sugar Ray somehow gets a main role too.
The cameos are more fun. On paper at least. Kelly Osbourne, Perez Hilton, Kurt Angle, Andy Dick and Billy Ray Cyrus all appear in what is a pretty

star studded cameo round up. Several of them meet a bloody end. Horror fans will be glad to see long time Scream Queen Tiffany Shelpis turn up.

Opening Scene: It's kind of fantastic! Fin Shepard (Ziering) and April Wexler (Reid) are on a plane. Fin notices sharks outside his window but thinks he must be imagining things. Of course he isn't and a sharknado soon appears ripping apart the plane. Sharks enter the plane, eating people and taking them apart, including Kelly Osbourne. But of course, Fin and April stay alive, somehow managing not to be sucked out of the giant hole in the plane. April is unlucky (or lucky?!) enough to lose half her arm when a shark rips it off despite her shooting at it over and over. Unfortunately, the pilots aren't as lucky and Fin has to land the plane himself, which he does surprisingly well.

Awfully Good performance: Vivica A. Fox is hilariously bad in her role. Of course it fits the film perfectly but you'll be surprised the actress was ever in Kill Bill and several other good movies.

Awfully Good line: *"You know what you just did don't ya?*
Don't say it.
You jumped the shark."
You guess what happened on screen just a few seconds before....

Awfully Good scene: This comes from the line above, when Fin (I have literally just realised why his name is Fin - get it?!), stranded on top of a taxi with water and sharks between him and safety. He unbelievably manages to jump from one shark leaping off of it to another and hops across a few more to safety. It's amazingly ridiculous.

Other notes and scenes: There's so many! A former baseball player hitting that final home run. Only he is hitting a shark straight out of the sky. The chainsaw into the shark scene steps it up a bit from the first one as Fin this time flies into the sharks mouth and out the back of it via a chainsaw in one swift motion, in mid-air. There's decapitations seemingly every few minutes with sharks biting the heads off of people. An axe is used to kill one swimming shark, directly in its face. Tara Reid gets in on the fun when she attaches a buzz saw to her half arm (in a very obvious nod to ash from Evil Dead, and not the only one). She then proceeds to slice into a shark mid air while it flies towards her. A giant baseball bat is used not very well to batter off a shark. Oh, and a shark manages to time his attack perfectly while Fin delivers his motivational speech to the city. Towards the end a shark comes flying at him but, in front of everyone, he starts up his chainsaw and beautifully saws the shark in half. An old guy feels the best way to sort things out is by launching old rusty chainsaws into the air (well into the sharknado). This kind of works a little, as does throwing mini bombs into it to. The Statue of Liberty even gets in on the action. Well it's head does. After the sharknado knocks it off, it causes havoc while rolling through the city. And this is all without mentioning the final scene.....

Final scene: It's a good one. Fin ends up riding a shark through the air! Holding on via a chain he manages to stand on top of it until the sharknado causes the shark to skewer itself on a pole on top of a skyscraper. But it's not finished there! When he then reaches April on top of the building they are lucky to be attacked by the shark that ate her arm (it must have been waiting for just the right moment). It is also somehow still holding her arm in its mouth. So when Fin shoots it down he takes out her arm, takes her wedding finger off of it and proposes again.

Final thoughts: Sharknado 2 is probably the most fun awfully good style film I've watched in a while. If you've never watched any of these types of films, watch this one. If you have, still watch this because you'll love it!

EIGHT LEGGED FREAKS (2002)

'Let the squashing begin!'

Synopsis: Venomous spiders get exposed to a noxious chemical that causes them to grow to monumental proportions.

Director: I'm not really sure what happened to Ellory Elkayem. Because after this entertaining noughties flick he made two DTV Return of the Living Dead movies (Necropolis and Rave to the Grave) and **a sequel** to Without A Paddle (Nature's Calling) and then nothing after 2009.

Cast: David Arquette is obviously pretty well known. Probably to horror fans from the Scream films. He seems to have had a bit of a career resurgence recently off of the back of him wrestling again and making a documentary on it - You Cannot Kill David Arquette and just because he seems like a genuinely nice guy. Kari Wuhrer has appeared in quite a few horror films including 1997's Anaconda and this years Sharknado 2: The Second One. Scott Terra hasn't done a whole lot since this film except for Daredevil. Scarlett Johansson on the other hand has had a half decent career since. Starring in a few films such as all the Avengers films, Black Widow, JoJo Rabbit, Sing, Jungle Book..... I could go on forever! Doug E. Doug (what kind of name is that) is best known for his role in Cool Runnings as Sanka. Rick Overton has had a busy career appearing in some well known films such as Groundhog Day and Cloverfield. While Matt Czuchry has had a decent TV career with The Good Wife and The Resident. Finally, Leon Rippy has done a lot of TV work including Deadwood, Saving Grace and Under the Dome.

Opening scene: Alot less exciting than most. We get a brief introduction by the crazy local radio DJ and then we follow a lorry driver. He swerves quickly while trying to avoid a rabbit, accidentally knocking a barrel off of his load. The barrel, containing some kind of toxic waste, lands in the river below.

Awfully Good character: It was a toss up between Deputy Pete Willis and Mayor Wade. But the deputy played by Rick Overton just about gets the nod. The character is quite stereotypical as the kinda dumb but amusing sidekick to the Sheriff. He's also involved in an amusing exchange of words with another character when he is asked "What exactly is it?" His reply, "It's a spider...man." Okay maybe it's a little funnier on screen.

Awfully Good line: I'm sure you're wondering what could beat the line above. Well this exchange does. ***"Lose the face fuzz before you do. It makes your mouth look like a strippers crotch."*** I think that's what it says at least, as a kettle boils to cover the last word.

Awfully Good scene: Towards the end of the film an old guy is holding a rifle, slowly walking through a shop while on high alert for any spiders. Behind him we see a tent move slightly. He looks behind but the tent is motionless. He carries on, only for us to see the tent move again. He checks again but nothing. A third time, and as he turns around a spider leaps from the tent, face hugging the old guy, Alien-style.

Other notes and scenes: The first time we see a spider really kill anyone, it's a cat that is the victim. But we don't really see much as it happens in the walls and ceiling of a house. The cats owners watch in horror as the cat is dragged about the inside of the wall, occasionally being splattered against the wall until it is electrocuted on the light fitting. The first real sight of a massive spider is actually really well shot and looks great, as it's lit from behind and down a mine. When we see down the mine, we are shown a worker sucking up things from a pipe. These things turn out to be spiders which we then see leave his mouth as he slowly opens it. Scarlett Johansson explains she doesn't want to lose her virginity in the back of the truck in a scene which ends with her using a tazer gun on her boyfriend's balls. Her boyfriend and his group of 'bikers' are then attacked and chased by the spiders. The chase scene shows several bikers die from jumping spiders, one guy does manage to kick one out mid flight. The chase ends when a lorry gets involved, which explodes and kills a few of the spiders. Many times people (and once a dog) are quickly whipped away by a spider. Sometimes we are lucky enough to see them comically whirl around while they get wrapped in a web. A spider manages to get in through Scarlett Johansson's bedroom window. It's easy to see what year this was made by looking at the nu-metal posters on her wall. Anyway, the spider shoots its web at her and David Arquette, only to be shot to its death with green goo (maybe blood) flowing out of it. There is one massive queen spider, who looks pretty impressive when she's on screen. One spider violently attacks a deer.....head, that is attached to a wall. There is a really cool shot of the hundreds of spiders walking towards the shopping mall, Dawn of the Dead-like. Oh, David Arquette does get to kind of zip wire into the mall, with, I think, a screaming spider trying to follow him down.

Final scene: There's lots of people running around underground tunnels trying to escape the spiders. But they can't use gunfire incase it sets off some gas in the mines. Arquette does fend one off with a tiny bug spray (while saving Gladdis). He then manages to get hold of a motorbike, luckily enough, because he is being chased by dozens of spiders including the queen. Of course he exits the tunnel as an explosion follows him and Gladdis out, jumping through the air while the spiders all die.

Final thoughts: Eight Legged Freaks is a bit of an Awfully Good 'classic'. The CGI doesn't look too bad even now at over twenty years old, it has a decent, now well known cast and is most importantly fun. If somehow you missed it first time round, go give it a watch.

NINJA ZOMBIES (2011)

'A new breed of ninjas are coming…'

Synopsis: In this raucous horror-comedy, a landlord must fight an army of undead ninjas after one of his tenants discovers an ancient sword of necromancy.

Director: This is the only movie from director Noah Cooper.

Cast: Unsurprisingly, if you've seen the film, almost all the actors in Ninja Zombies don't seem to have done anything else. But there are a few exceptions. Duc Nguyen has randomly done voice work in a few anime films in the late nineties and Arun Storrs has since worked on films called The Worst Year of My Life and Finding Emma. The biggest surprise though is that Lloyd Kauffman (creator of Troma) has a cameo! I have no idea how this happens.

Opening scene: Some guy is in a forest and he starts fighting a girl. Soon enough, swords are out and it therefore becomes a sword fight! One of the swords is a hell sword apparently. I'm not sure what that is. But ninjas then start to attack so it might be useful. There's lots of fighting, lots of blood sprayed across the screen and then a guy wakes up in his bed and the opening credits start.

Awfully Good character: Well, there's two. The two best friends and the two 'jocks' of the group. They're basically two overweight guys who say sexual innuendos throughout most the film. Awfully (occasionally awfully good) scripted lines, several that will be mentioned later in the review. They call each other 'dog' and their best line is the overly used but still quite funny "That's what she said". Their friendship is ended when one has to kill the other when he becomes a zombie. He does this with a baseball bat while sobbing about how sorry he is.

Awfully Good line: I'm not sure how 'good' this line is but **"Maybe you**

should stop sucking your mother's dong" is an insult I had not heard before.

Awfully Good scene: It's a flashback scene. One character's brother is shown hitting mailboxes with a baseball bat. The car swerves and he falls out, impaling himself on a mailbox. We don't actually see this but we do see a wave of red liquid that is supposed to blood, cover some onlookers.

Other notes and scenes: There's a fight scene with plastic swords that is meant as a bit of a joke but might be the most well shot scene in the whole film. The ninjas fighting in the forest crops up several more times. The forest is also home to a magic ritual spell which one girl performs to bring back her dead brother. Obviously it goes horribly wrong and she brings back some ninja zombies aswell. Her brother didn't last long until he was killed again either. This time, he met his end with a baseball bat. The second zombie attack is on a woman who thinks the best way to defend herself is by throwing her clothes at it. Part of the ninjas back story is told through a small amount of animation, which might just be the best part of the film. We are shown a few clips of the zombies going on a killing spree through the town. They kill about five people. The film makers obviously thought having blood splatter all over the camera was a good idea because it happens in every fight scene. Despite having brutal deaths, the director didn't seem to want anyone using the word fuck. Instead phrases like "What the F", "Mother-F-ing" and "What the frack", are used. Without a decent budget, killing someone by sword can be difficult to make look good. Unfortunately, to counter this in Ninja Zombies, the old 'weapon under the armpit trick' is used. Not to very good effect. The script is so Awfully Good at times. When we enter a character's mind he asks why a person in his mind is speaking English, when he couldn't in the real world. The reply was something close to "I'm not speaking English.....your mind is hearing English"! Another actual highlight was the decapitation of Trish, which actually looked great. Lloyd Kauffman actually steals the film with his cameo. A crazier (I assume) version of himself. He has more charisma than the rest of the cast put together. Before the final scenes we have two characters go through a change of clothes montage. The main character decided his best ninja zombie fighting outfit was a tight white sleeveless hoody.

Final scene: We're back in the forest. There's a lot of zombies, well quite a lot. The remaining few characters fight them off with some poor fighting, until it comes down to a one on one fight with our main 'hero' and a ninja zombie. He kills the zombie off relatively easy and with one swipe of a sword, the zombie kind of disappears. The couple that have been teasing getting together hold hands and walk off with the hero. But that's not really the end. They decide to go off looking for more zombies to kill.

Final thoughts: Ninja Zombies is strangely entertaining. It's not very good and I assume it's made by friends and students who somehow got Lloyd Kauffman involved. A film called Ninja Zombies has plenty of potential, I think. Or maybe it's just not a very good idea. It doesn't seem like a good idea after watching this film.

SNOWBEAST (1977)

'An unknown terror stalks the ski resort!'

Synopsis: A Colorado ski resort is besieged by a sub-human beast that commits brutal murders on the slopes.

Director: Herb Wallerstein directed episodes of TV for Wonder Woman, Happy Days and Star Trek.

Cast: Bo Svenson has also appeared in the Tarantino films, Inglorious Basterds and Kill Bill Vol. 2. Yvette Mimeux starred in the sci-fi films The Time Machine, The Black Hole
and Dark of the Sun. Clint Walker's last film role was the voice of Nick Nitro in Small Soldiers. Sylvia Sidney appeared in the Tim Burton films Beetlejuice and Mars Attacks! Thomas Babson had a role in another beast film called, erm, Beasts. Which also starred Snowbeast co-star Kathy Christopher.

Opening scene: The film starts with a snow covered landscape and snow covered trees. With an actually pretty good horror score playing. The credits are rolling as we suddenly see the arm of a beast appear and its hand grab a branch.

Awfully Good character: There's not much in the way of comic relief in these characters. So the Snowbeast itself gets this honour. I'm not completely sure what it looks like because we never really see it clearly. The viewer gets to see a lot of its arm. I guess it's mainly a Bigfoot-like creature.

Awfully Good line: Again, not a whole lot of clever lines here, but this did get a smirk from me. When talking about the Snowbeast.....
"This wasn't an animal and it wasn't a human either"
"Well that narrows things down."

Awfully Good scene: The first proper sighting of the Snowbeast's face is as entertaining as the film gets. One character's face suddenly changes to fear as the camera zooms in on her. The camera then pans around to a nearby window and the viewer gets a quick glimpse of the beast's face! There's panic in the hall that the beast is outside of but a car arrives that distracts the beast. Unfortunately for the women inside the car, the beast attacks her. Smashing the window and leaving her a bloody mess. We don't actually get to see what it does, just the aftermath when the police arrive.

Other notes and scenes: Snowbeast features a lot of scenes of people skiing. Just skiing down slopes. And then a bit later in the film, this changes to snowmobiles. The skiing is normally accompanied with happy music. Snowbeast is similar to Bigfoot in more ways than just its appearance. It's also hardly ever seen. We see its footprints and stupid people usually follow these for some reason. We also hear it roar a lot too. A couple of people fall while skiing in the least convincing way I have ever seen. This is obviously while the beast is chasing them. Towards the films end we have four 'heroes' out to kill the beast. One is soon killed off when the beast rolls some cut down tress towards their camper van while he's inside. Every 'death' scene ends with a close up of the victim paused as the screen turns red.

Final scene: The final three find a gun and start shooting at the beast. It doesn't effect the beast much so they go chasing it, pretty slowly, on skis. We finally get a decent view of the beasts face (it wasn't worth the wait) as it attacks. The continued shooting doesn't work but a ski held straight against a tree trunk, does the trick when it stabs the beast who then stumbles back and falls down a (not that steep) cliff to, what I assume is, its death.

Final thoughts: Made over 40 years ago, more recent Awfully Good films are a bit more exciting. This has a slow pace that never really picks up and I actually prefer the remake made in 2011. Snowbeast isn't awful but it's not much fun either.

WOLF TOWN (2011)

'Hungry, vicious, deadly'

Synopsis: Kyle, a shy college student finds himself and three of his friends trapped in an old western ghost town by a pack of ferocious wolves and has to overcome his personal fears to confront the wolves and lead his friends to safety.

Director: John Rebel seems to have changed his name and is now known as Roel Reine - Under the name John Rebel he directed Wolf Town and Bear and strangely as Rebel Wan he directed Deadwater. Otherwise he has directed The Marine 2, Death Race 2 & 3, The Scorpion King 3: Battle For Redemption, 12 Rounds 2: Reloaded, The Man With The Iron Fists 2 and The Condemned - a man of many sequels!

Cast: Alicia Zielgler has also starred in Rise of the Dinosaurs, Jurassic Attack and Lake Placid 2. Levi Fiehler has appeared in Puppet Master: Axis of Evil and an episode of Twisted Tales, while recently appearing as the Mayor in Resident Alien. Max Adler is best known for playing Dave Karofsky in Glee but also played a zombie in an episode of Big Bang Theory and bigger roles in Flash and Sully. Josh Kelly's biggest roles to date were in the two Transformers films, Revenge of the Fallen and Dark of the Moon. Brilliantly, on IMDb the Wolves get a cast credit as 'themselves'!

Opening scene: Nothing much happens. The credits role and the setting behind is an old western town. A group of old guys gather and load their guns. Meanwhile, a child lays at the door of a families home, presumably dead, with blood surrounding him.
As the credits finish, we start in present day as a guy wakes up late to meet his best friend.

Awfully Good character: As they have an IMDb credit, it has to go to the wolves. They are very intelligent wolves including, I assume, biting through car wires so their victims couldn't escape via car. They are the highlight of the film.

Awfully Good line: *"You wanna go out here and let the wolves know we're not coming back?".*
Maybe they should have tried this? They were pretty intelligent wolves after all.

Awfully Good scene: I'll ignore the wolves cutting the wires and go with the scene when our main characters have boarded themselves into a building. I'm not sure how but one wolf manages to get in via the upstairs floor. It was possibly always there. It slowly walks down the stairs while our group of friends just stand there watching it. It continues around as they kind of follow it while it walks up on to a bar area. The group still looking at it from about two metres away have a bit of a stare down while nothing happens. The wolf then leaps on to one of the guys. Unfortunately, the guy comes out on top when he beats the wolf to death. We get this death in slow motion with the guy spitting at the camera for some reason.

Other notes and scenes: Despite being intelligent, some of the wolves seem to be deaf or blind or both. One scene sees a character bring a massive ladder to the side of a building, a few feet from two wolves. He places the ladder against the building and climbs up, but they don't even flinch. At one point the lead female believes that moving very slowly will stop the wolves attacking - possibly like that scene with Drax in Guardians of the Galaxy 2. It doesn't work, obviously, but it would have been an interesting (maybe) film if it did. One of the scenes when the wolves were being prodded at with tree trunks from one guy, just looked like a dog playing with a big stick. Another time, the wolves were eating the flesh of one of its victims. Except, the 'flesh' was clearly strips of bacon. The majority of the time, the wolves looked pretty friendly and not at all like the violent killers they were supposed to be. When one girl has her leg bitten, it is bandaged extremely badly by her male friend. It looked more like some kind of fashion statement strapped to her leg. Of course, there's a love story here. The girl who has a boyfriend but also a best friend that was never brave enough to ask her out. Unfortunately, the boyfriend seems like a decent enough guy, with good ideas to survive this situation. Whereas the best friend is useless because he was attacked by a dog when he was younger. He spends quite a bit of time just crying and is generally a bit of a loser. Oh, and there's only two wolves around for most of the film.

I think six of them are seen for one brief moment together but otherwise this is a very small 'group' or skulk - I learnt that would for this piece.

Final scene: Luckily, there happens to be some dynamite lying about. So they decide this is the best way to defeat the wolves. The boyfriend doesn't make it to the end when he is attacked and eaten by the wolves while trying to start this plan. There's a brilliant moment when our final two characters look through the cracks in the cabin they are in, out at the wolves, despite being three inches from a giant window that they could look out of. The best friend manages to lure the wolves into a building with the dynamite, while throwing a lighter at it as he runs up the stairs and is blown outside by the explosion. He is somehow uninjured by this. One wolf survives but soon lets the new couple leave when the guy waves a stick of dynamite at him. The wolf gets the hint and leaves them alone.

Final thoughts: Wolf Town is pretty awful in the best possible way. There's a cheesy love story, an explosion and killer animals. Unfortunately no poor CGI but Awfully Good fans will still enjoy.

OCTOPUS 2: RIVER OF FEAR (2001)

'Out of time... out of breath!'

Synopsis: A giant, man-eating octopus suddenly appears in the Hudson River during the Fourth of July weekend and begins to leave a trail of dead bodies behind it.

Director: Yossi Wein has a list of action and disaster films to his name including Cyborg Cop III, Death Train and Disaster. His last movie was 2003s Sudden Damage.

Cast: Michael Reilly Burke has been more successful than most Awfully Good actors. He played Ted Bundy in Bundy and has also starred in The Collector, Slender Man and Mars Attacks! Meredith Morton appeared in the fantastically titled Alien Fury: Countdown to Invasion. Fredric Lehne has mainly done TV work, including The X-Files, Dexter: New Blood and American Horror Story: Asylum. But he's also appeared in some big time movies including Men in Black, The Greatest Showman and Dark Knight Rises. Shortly after Octopus 2, John Thaddeus appeared in Firefly and Charmed. Chris Williams' biggest film role came in Dodgeball but he also played Hoover in Silicon Valley. Clement Blake has played 'homeless man' in at least five films including this one. Finally Duncan Fraser starred in The Exorcism of Emily Rose, The Hitcher II: I've Been Waiting, The Predator, The Haunting of Bly Manor and Omen IV: The Awakening.

Opening scene: We see New York in the background and then a drunk couple on the edge of a river. The guy is more drunk than the woman. He stumbles into a nearby rowing boat and is soon grabbed by an octopus tentacle. After a brief struggle he is taken underwater. The woman is standing nearby and screaming, and is also taken underwater to her death by another tentacle.

Awfully Good character: This might be just for his name but it's 'Mad Dog'. He's played by Clement Blake who once again, as mentioned above, plays a homeless guy. He is the first to tell the police that there is a killer octopus on the loose but for some reason (probably because he's drunk and called Mad Dog), they don't believe him.

Awfully Good line: It's not a film for catchy quotes but I quite liked *"land of the free, home of the sea monster"*. Actually would have made a good tagline.

Awfully Good scene: Unfortunately this scene was a dream sequence but it was still great. The octopus climbs up the Statue of Liberty in some Awfully Good CGI. The camera goes to close-ups of the people in the Statue at the very top. Including our main character Nick. As the octopus starts to pull the head from the statue, Nick falls, comically with more bad CGI, to the ground. But then the scene jumps to Nick waking up in bed.

Other notes and scenes: Somebody gets arrested underwater early on. That's a first for me and my film watching. There's actually some decent practical effects including the octopus's tentacles but this is alongside some really bad CGI effects. Considering the size of the octopus it somehow knows how to go straight for the neck of humans and strangle them to death. The octopus looks a lot like Godzilla when he's just got his head poking out of the water. Of the many weapons used, the big crane and claw thing is my favourite. Although it didn't actually work aswell as stabbing the thing with a small knife. Once again, the film involves a love story. Our main guy Nick gets involved with the Mayor's secretary. The mayor is mentioned so much just to be some kind of bad guy who doesn't care much about a giant octopus destroying his city.

Final scene: The final ten minutes or more should be classed as the final 'scene'. It's a strange last quarter of an hour because it feels like it was just added on because killing the octopus wasn't exciting enough. Because after that happens, there's a whole lot of drama, starting with a car crash in a tunnel that before its death, the octopus started destroying. To make this as tense filled as possible, there's a bus full of children, including a girl in a wheelchair, an old woman and a dog! They desperately want Nick to be a hero. There's a lot of explosions, water leaking in and parts of the tunnel falling everywhere. The old woman (who I think is quite a young woman in a grey wig) is saved, and then her dog is. Nick then returns to save all the children one by one, lastly the girl in the wheelchair by carrying her on his back and climbing up a ladder. It all feels like it's out of a different movie and it actually looks quite expensive. When everybody has climbed the ladder to safety the octopus suddenly reappears! But it lasts a matter of seconds when it is shot at and there's a big explosion as I assume it dies. All the children cheer and everybody is happy.

Final thoughts: This sequel is an improvement on the first film and is quite entertaining in a weird way. And that final scene could be straight out of some nineties action film. Bring on Octopus 3 (maybe).

GOBLIN (2010)

'He wants you badly'

Synopsis: Every Halloween, a small hamlet in the deep woods is visited by a fierce goblin, intent on capturing infants and brutally murdering anyone in its path.

Director: Jeffrey Scott Lando has also directed Roboshark, Boogeyman, Dead of Night and House of Bones. His most recent film is 2022's Lissa's Trip - a story about an actress accidentally taking acid before a big audition.

Cast: Gil Bellows is a very experienced actor who usually puts in good performances including The Shawshank Redemption and more recently in Extraterrestrial. In the last few years he has appeared in Scary Stories To Tell In The Dark and the show American Gods. Tracy Spiridakos has recently appeared in TV shows Being Human, Chicago P.D. and Bates Motel. Camille Sullivan has appeared in The Butterfly Effect and The Marine 3: Homefront. Her more recent horror C.V. includes Dead Rising: Endgame, Hunter Hunter and Harland Manor. Brett Dier has starred in horror films such as Grace, and Exeter but is best known as Michael in Jane the Virgin. Colin Cunningham has been in the TV shows The X-Files and Falling Skies and has plenty of horror to his name, including Blood Drive and Curse of Crom: The Legend of Halloween. Andrew Wheeler had a role in The Exorcism of Emily Rose, as well as blockbuster The Day the Earth Stood Still. In the last five years he has had roles in the shows iZombie, Riverdale and Supergirl. Reilly Dolman has starred in Mega Cyclone, Scarecrow and the 2019 creepy show based on a book - The Terror. Donnelly Rhodes has acted in films as varied as Butch Cassidy and the Sundance Kid and TRON: Legacy.

Opening scene: The credits run with a fire in the background. And we are told this is Halloween night 1831. People are around a fire in a forest, when we discover they are 'burning the unclean'. This shockingly means that they are killing babies. Then, a baby is thrown into the fire! The mother of this baby turns out to be a witch. Why she didn't use this to stop her child being killed I don't know. Instead she now casts a spell on the village that summons a goblin from the flames. The goblin then kills a woman and its baby.

Awfully Good character: Everybody likes the crazy old guy in these movies. Here, he is played by Donnelly Rhodes and like in a lot of these films, he is usually right about things but everyone thinks he's just crazy. Partly because he's normally drunk.

Awfully Good line: *"Sounds like a caffeine hallucination"*. Which I had to look up and apparently it is a real thing. As you can see, this wasn't a movie full of great one-liners.

Awfully Good scene: It's more of a moment but when a sheriff and his deputy have a brief dispute and pull their guns on each other, the film suddenly goes into slow motion. The deputy is unfortunately the one who loses his life.

Other notes and scenes: The goblin looks like Death, just with a goblins face, for the most part of the film. He wears a big black robe with a hood and moves from one place to another by kind of disappearing into his robe and flying about in awful CGI. The mother is killed when the goblin smashes a glass door and one large piece stabs her. The goblin smells really bad apparently. In fact that's how the characters know if it is nearby. One character starts throwing up before he realises the goblin is stood behind him. By far the best death scene then follows when the goblin claps his hands together, with the guys head in between, it nearly explodes and blood goes everywhere. The old crazy guy of course has the only weapon that can kill the goblin. But the sheriff and his wife think it's a better idea to sacrifice a baby and end the towns curse. Also believing this will somehow return their son that they believe the goblin has.

Final scene: The father of the child that the goblin is after, shoots at the goblin. Some kind of ghosts whizz around the goblin and he then throws his robe off and we see him in all his glory for the first time. It then cuts open Charlie (the crazy old guy) by just scratching him with its claws constantly while blood sprays out. The sheriff shoots at it but this just leads to him and his wife both being killed pretty quickly in a similar way.

The father of the baby the Goblin wants, his daughter and her boyfriend, and the baby then wait in a house for him to appear and hopefully be killed. They soon smell him and he bursts into the house, slitting the throat of the boyfriend. The daughter runs away but has the only weapon that can kill the goblin, a spear. She attaches it to a car and drives at the goblin, spearing it through its body and against a tree. And that's that.

Final thoughts: Goblin wasn't quite as exciting as I hoped. The goblin should have been more violent and killing more people. More death and blood would have livened things up a bit. It's not completely dull but is nothing more than watchable for the most part.

STONADOS (2013)

'A stones throw to disaster'

Synopsis: When a tornado appears in the waters south of Boston, former storm chaser Joe Randall is intrigued by the unusual weather. But as twisters begin to strike across the Boston shoreline, Joe quickly realizes this is no ordinary storm front.

Director: Jason Bourque currently has 53 directing credits to his name including 2017 movie Drone starring Sean Bean. He seems to be another director who has settled in to regular straight to TV Christmas movies, including, The Tale of Two Christmasses, My Favourite Christmas Tree and The Christmas Retreat.

Cast: Paul Johansson played Dan Scott in One Tree Hill and also appeared in the remake of Carnival of Souls. More recently he played Dmitri in the TV series Van Helsing. Miranda Frigon starred in White Noise aswell as episodes of The Dead Zone, Dexter, Primeval: New World, Supernatural and the recent Day of the Dead. Jessica McLeod appeared in Scary Movie 4 and R.L. Stine's The Haunting Hour, while also starring in Van Helsing and Netflix hit Brand New Cherry Flavour. Dylan Scmid was also part of The Haunting Hour and an episode of Falling Skies. His latest role being one of his biggest as Patterson in the Snowpiercer series. William B. Davis is of course best known for his role of cigarette smoking man in The X-Files but lately has been scaring people in the Chilling Adventures of Sabrina and The Midnight Club. Aliyah O'Brien starred in several episodes of Bate's Motel, Insomnia and Legends of Tomorrow. While Josh Byer's appearances range from a small role in Night of the Museum: Battle of Smithsonian to a bigger role in low budget horror, Ripper and four episodes of superhero show Arrow. Dominika Julliet has starred in the brilliantly titled Dragon Wasps and Dracano. Sebastian Spence has had a long career mainly in TV, including Battlestar Galactica, Cedar Cove and American Gods. Part actor part stunt guy, Dalius Blake has appeared in

Superman and Louis, X-Men Origins: Wolverine and Elysium. Another stunt guy, Hugo Steele has worked on the movie that turned me Vegan, Okja, Watchmen and Star Trek Beyond.

Opening scene: A tour guide is showing some tourists around Plymouth Rock. The wind starts to pick up and a tornado can be seen in the distance at sea. One tourist asks "What is that?". Obviously not a very intelligent tourist. While trying to hold on to whatever she can, the tour guide gets swept away into the tornado and then it suddenly stops.

Awfully Good character: The street psychic gets this prize. She runs up to one of the main characters in the middle of a storm and shouts "aren't you off TV?!". He tells her he is, so she starts to slag him off and blames him for the current stonado that is happening. Moments later she is flattened by a giant rock.

Awfully Good line: Delivered by a friend of the daughter of one of the main characters. She complains to her male companion, *"It's raining rocks and we're hiding behind a plastic table!"*. She has a point.

Awfully Good scene: A rock has crashed through the roof of a car. Our three main characters are looking at it. One of them, despite knowing what will happen, touches it and burns himself. But then the rock starts shaking. The tension is building, well its suppose to but the close-ups of peoples faces and then the rock didn't really do it for me. The rock then explodes in the car. Not a huge explosion but it does some damage.

Other notes and scenes: Incase you weren't sure, a stonado looks a lot like a tornado. There's a few things the viewer gets to see an awful lot of during Stonados.
1 - people running away in slow motion, 2 - poor CGI and 3 - people talking about the weather using words you don't understand.
The running about panicking is the most heavily featured. One guy leaps over the middle guard rail of a staircase for absolutely no reason. In fact it hindered his escape from the storm more than helped him. When three people run to a van that they are all getting into, one character throws the keys to another and they are dropped and lost briefly as the stonado heads towards them! Surely just keep hold of the keys and hand them to him in the van. A giant swan style paddle boat is taken out by a rock and is top of the list of fun things taken out by the stonados. One cameraman does unfortunately get taken out by one of the exploding rocks. One moment

shows people shouting and running as they look out at sea at a stonado but a rower who is much nearer the actual stonado is just casually rowing along. A lighthouse is taken out by stones and falls on an old man. One of my favourite moments involves a close-up of a normal looking sky with dramatic music. I assume this is hinting at a future stonado. The shaking rocks attempt to bring some more tension when a van is driven badly through a street of them. One girl is hit by some stones and does a beautiful somersault over a railing. A basketball player is randomly taken out by another rock mid-game.

Final scene: The idea is to bomb a cloud. Or something like that. The stonado is flying through the city. To get the bomb to the stonado, the 'heroes' decide to drive a car with all their family and friends in and the bomb. Not the plan I would have gone for. The only kind of 'villain' of the film apologises for not believing that stonados existed and then gets destroyed by a rock. Oh, they bought a bazooka with them too but that didn't work. So they just all got out of the car and let the stonado take it away and it explodes and stops everything. Thus, leaving everybody smiling.

Final thoughts: Not quite as cool as Sharknado but fans of that film and Awfully Good films in general will get plenty of enjoyment from Stonados.

MONSTERWOLF (2010)

'They must fight for their lives'

Synopsis: A group of people who represent an oil company find new ground to drill for oil but then accidentally unleash a wolf-like creature. The creature wreaks havoc in the town and can only be stopped by the last surviving native American.

Director: Todor Chapkanov has also directed Ghost Town (not the Ricky Gervais one) and Storm War. He's still busy and in 2023 directed Frank Grillo in Black Lotus. He has also worked as first assistant director on 2022's excellent horror Barbarian and The Hitman's Bodyguard.

Cast: Before Monsterwolf, Lenor Varela starred in Blade 2 and Hell Ride. The most interesting movie she has been in since, is probably Odd Thomas. Robert Picardo's work ranges from Gremlins 2 to Mega Shark vs. Crocosaurus but will be best known for playing The Doctor in Star Trek: Voyager. In more recent years he appeared in Hail, Caesar!, The Flash and the new series of Quantum Leap. Marc Macaulay has 143 credits to his IMDb name including 12 Years a Slave, Bad Boys and Edward Scissorhands. Steve Reevis has gone from Fargo to Malcolm in the Middle. Ricky Wayne has appeared in several horror related projects including The Town That Dreaded Sundown remake and several episodes of The Walking Dead. He also has the distinction of playing Adolf Hitler (in the TV series 'Your Pretty Face Is Going To Hell). Griff Furst has starred in films as big as The Green Lantern and Terminator Genisys but also Atomic Shark. Jon Eyez also has some well known films to his name including Django Unchained, Logan Lucky, Dawn of the Planet of the Apes and four episodes of The Walking Dead. Jason London appeared in a future Awfully Good reviewed film, Zombie Shark. Grant James has also featured in 184 TV and films including Better Call Saul, Arachnoquake and Dumb and Dumber To. Nicole Barre hasn't worked for a few years but played Kathy in ten episodes of The Walking Dead.

Opening scene: A group of oil workers dig up a flame floating in the air. It is surrounded by some sort of artefact so they ring their boss about what to do about it. They are told to blow it up. Obviously. They try, but appearing from the smoke is a wolf. A very big wolf. A Monsterwolf we assume. It leaps over a big metal fence and rips apart several workers with a bit of blood spraying everywhere.

Awfully Good character: The self-proclaimed 'hard-ass' is the boss of the oil company. He doesn't really care about anybody or anything as long as his company is making money. He also doesn't believe it's a Monsterwolf killing all these people. Which is actually fair enough even if he's wrong. But when he does know about it he hires a gang of killers. People that kill humans but I guess there as good as anybody to kill a Monsterwolf.

Awfully Good line: A Native American characters tells some people that he saw them coming. When asked if he saw this in a dream, he replies with **"No, I saw you through the window"**. Delivered nicely, it actually made me chuckle.

Awfully Good scene: A woman is stuck inside a house with the wolf inside and after her. She decides to call her ex for help. Even before she calls the police or her father who is a police officer. She is eventually helped as a guy shoots the wolf but it somehow stays alive. The woman keeps running away and she's very fast because the wolf can't catch up. The wolf eventually gets taken out by a truck but does not die.

Other notes and scenes: The Monsterwolf is a spirit that is defending the town from the evil oil company, so it is killing everyone involved in that project. I'm not sure how the wolf knows who this is but it does. There are a couple of brief practical effects used for the wolf but it's mostly awful CGI. There is a love story that is in about 75% of Awfully Good films. A woman has left the town she grew up in, usually for her career, and therefore left her childhood sweetheart who probably doesn't want to leave his redneck town. She is now back, in this film as a lawyer for the oil company but she hasn't told anyone. So she first bumps into her father and then her ex who she eventually falls in love with again and they live happily ever after. The team that are hired to kill the wolf by the oil company boss, seem to have arrived straight from The Predator. The main guy with a cigar in his mouth, obviously everyone in camouflage and using something that's not quite heat vision. One of them does come equipped with a horn that sounds out a wolf mating call. Which unsurprisingly doesn't help. To kill the wolf it needs to be with the bone of an enemy and exchanged a life for a life. One character has one of the best mullets to have ever graced a film and he wears a t-shirt that says HOLY CARP. Which got a laugh from me.

Final scene: Well this starts with perhaps the best moment of the film as the wolf leaps at a helicopter that is several dozen feet above the ground and there's a big explosion. Which I thought killed the wolf but it survived. It takes it time to attack the main boss and is then killed with a weird speaking thing which presumably has the bone of enemy in it. It disappears as the woman collapses. But we fast forward....well, I'm not sure how long forward, but the childhood sweethearts are soon to be married. Not only are they happy with that but they place the wolf's ashes back into the artefact until someone else attacks the towns residents.

Final thoughts: Monsterwolf is a fun enough Awfully Good film that does nothing new or original to impress but nonetheless is entertaining for the most part.

JURASSIC CROC (AKA SUPERCROC) (2007)

*'It's 50 feet long... It's 25 feet tall...
And in 14 hours it will be here!'*

Synopsis: A team of soldiers must stop a giant, bloodthirsty crocodile from reaching a nearby city, while trying to avoid being a meal for the beast themselves.

Director: Scott Harper only directed this and Alien Vs. Hunter. But he did work on the visual effects for films such as Snakes on a Plane and Ghost Ship.

Cast: Cynthia Rose Hall hasn't had many roles but has appeared in the TV shows Agents of S.H.I.E.L.D. and Sons of Anarchy. Kim Little has appeared in a few horror films with great titles including Scarecrow Slayer, Death Valley: The Revenge of Bloody Bill, The Last Sharknado: It's About Time and a couple of episodes of the zombie show Z Nation. David Novak also starred in Super Shark! Jurassic Croc was Kristen Quintrall's first role and she has gone on to do lots more low budget sci-fi and horror such as Invasion of the Pod People and Transmorphers but nothing since 2012. Noel Thurman had to fight off more horrible things in 2017s Piranha Sharks but maybe that was enough for her because she hasn't been seen acting since.

Opening scene: This is unfortunately alot slower paced and longer than most. While the opening credits run, an army are trekking through some woodland until they reach a lake. There's a close up of one guy when we see a giant crocodiles eyes and opening mouth. A splash in the water later and here's gone. Nothing to exciting and it lasts about nine minutes.

Awfully Good character: Dr. Leah Perrot played by Kim Little. She just seems to make up information on the crocodile because she's never really sure what it is. She is apparently a forensic palaeontologist. I'm not really sure whether she was helpful or unhelpful to the army and nor are they.

Awfully Good line: Spoken by Pvt. Celia Perez. *"What kinda bullet pissing jarhead moron can't tell the difference between a engagement ring and a wedding ring."* Well me actually, I'm pretty sure I couldn't.

Awfully Good scene: This scene should have been alot better than it was. It involves a helicopter being bitten out of the air by the giant crocodile! It takes the crocodile a while after it bites it. People look on in astonishment and eventually it brings the helicopter out with a crash, flames bellowing from the destruction.

Other notes and scenes: The crocodile comes back and chases the main female character but it appears that for a 50ft crocodile, it's not that fast. And she escapes by climbing a tree. There's several scenes that involve top army people and government officials in a room with screens and buttons. They chat alot and say things that mean nothing, like "we need to get a C-R-R straight away or the P-I-D's will be in trouble". This isn't an actual quote. Like many of the monsters in these Awfully Good films, the giant crocodile can still manage to sneak up on people unnoticed. The army also claim that they can't track the crocodile when it's on its where to the city. They can't track a 50ft crocodile walking through woodland! The croc eventually reaches the city and the army continue to shoot at it with hand guns despite it consistently having no effect. The army do manage to lure it where they want by using its eggs. A missile attack is attempted but seems to have no effect. Also, maybe I wasn't paying attention but as there were eggs, surely there is both a male and female croc about?! I don't think this was mentioned. When in the city, the croc stamps on a few people and on a random car that seemingly drove towards it instead of away for no reason.

Final scene: Once the croc is where they want it, one army guy goes to attach a bomb to its underbelly (it's weak spot). But he apparently gets knocked over by the crocodiles tail. I say apparently because it looked like it missed with his awful looking ducking and diving away from it. But anyway, this meant Pvt. Celia Perez had to save the day. She, surprisingly easily, walks up to the belly of the crocodile, attaches the bomb, and walks away uninjured. I think the croc had just given up to be honest. The bomb explodes and the Jurassic Croc is dead.........but! The camera pans round to a dumpster and we see a giant crocodile egg about to hatch.....

Final thoughts: Jurassic Croc was surprisingly tedious. I can't really really recommend it.

SHARKNADO 3: OH HELL NO! (2015)

'Oh hell no!' (apparently part of the title and the tagline)

Synopsis: A monstrous tornado unleashes ravenous sharks from Washington, D.C., all the way down to Orlando, Florida.

Director: Anthony C. Ferante hasn't been quite so interesting since the Sharknado movies, although he did direct Zombie Tidal Wave. His last two films were Butch Cassidy and the Wild Bunch and Crown Prince of Christmas.

Cast: So Ian Zeiring and Tara Reid are in all the Sharknado films - check out the first two entries to see their career highlights. Despite appearing in Bering Sea Beast and Sharknado in 2013, Cassie Scerbo missed out on Sharknado 2 before appearing in all the other sequels. Last year she starred in Requien For A Scream. Frankie Muniz is best known for playing Malcolm in Malcolm in the Middle. His 2018 genre movie - The Black String - is definitely worth checking out though. Ryan Newman's first film role was the voice of 'Little Girl' in Monster House and she continued in Sharknado 4, 5 & 6. David Hasselhoff is probably still best known for Baywatch and Knightrider, despite featuring in many other TV and film roles. He usually plays himself and somehow got to do that for Guardians of the Galaxy 2. Christopher Judge has starred in many episodes of Stargate as well as the great Mega Shark vs Mecha Shark. He's also done a lot of voice , including Kratos in God of War and it's follow-up. The fantastically named Diana Terranova also starred in Camel Spiders, Snake Outta Compton and Piranhaconda. Unknown to me, Mark Cuban is well known in America as a TV personality and businessman. Here, he plays the President. Bo Derek will always been known as Jenny in 10. She shows up in the last Sharknado movie too. There are of course many cameos. Musician Ne-Yo, wrestler and singer Chris Jericho, singers (and now social media celebrities) Jedward (I'm sure no-one in America knew who they were), singer Mark McGrath is back again, even Hulk himself Lou Ferrigno makes an appearance. Jerry Springer made an appearance without me even noticing. And Jackie Collins also makes a brief appearance. As do Penn and Teller, George R. R. Martin and Maryse Mizanin - there's too many to mention everybody!

Opening scene: It's a very long opening scene! Straight off, we have a James Bond-like intro but instead of a gun, the guy is holding a chainsaw. Then we see our main guy, Fin, doing a lot of running. A storm is coming and the President needs him! He phones April (Reid), who is now pregnant. He is making his way to collect his Medal of Freedom Award and some kind of new Golden Chainsaw award! As he does, he gets to meet a fan, Lou Ferrigno, who also gets to utter the line "Don't make me angry". Jackie Collins offers to write Fin's biography just before the sharks start to fly into the building. The golden chainsaw then comes in handy, cutting sharks in half. This sharknado produces one of the best moments from all three films as two characters surfboard down a water and shark covered staircase on paintings taken straight from the White House's walls. The President is trying to get to his underground bunker but the sharks of course get there first. This President though is ready to fight back. And alongside Fin, they use guns and grenades to take out the sharks. Blood sprays everywhere and they get out just before the White House is destroyed. But before the credits role, several characters work together to spike a shark on a flag pole holding the American flag.

Awfully Good character: I've mentioned him a lot above but I did enjoy The President played by Mark Cuban. A kick-ass, gun wielding President of America is as hilarious and Awfully Good as it sounds.

Awfully Good line: Sharknado 3 was unfortunately lacking in clever lines and puns. There was one scene where a character is definitely dead (I will talk about it more later). But the cries of Nova (Scerbo) are replied with ***"it's too late, we can't save him"***. I'm not sure why she didn't realise this herself after her friend was blown to bits in an explosion.

Awfully Good scene: This scene connects nicely with the line above. Lucas Stevens (Muniz) leaves Fin and Nova to fly away and save the world, while he just defends the place from an oncoming Sharknado. He doesn't last long without back-up though. A flying shark soon bites his leg off but he hops towards the truck he needs to get to. Unfortunately his arm is then bitten off. But he still manages to climb on top of the truck only for his other leg to be bitten off! But he still has one arm and hand to press the button he is aiming for. As he reaches to press it, his other arm is bitten off!! He's still moving and presses the button with his chin. This button sets off a massive explosion killing him and many sharks.

Other notes and scenes: A fognado even happens in this film. Maybe that's a title for a spin-off? As well as tornadoes, the sharks manage to take rides on water slides and hilariously on a rollercoaster. They even take part in a NASCAR race. The funniest moment in the film comes when Fin and Nova crash a plane into some water. They escape, alive, and somehow only wearing their underwear as they, in slow motion, appear from the water. A cinema screen isn't even safe, as a crowd watching what looks to be 3-Headed Shark Attack, are attacked themselves when a shark flies through the screen. The main group of characters survive one attack inside a giant Universal logo globe that bounces about the place. How they survived and how they got out of it when it lands on a very tall attraction is anybodies guess. It is not explained.

Final scene: Hasselhoff is heavily involved as he and his son, Fin, joined by April, head for space in a shuttle to do something with a giant bomb of sorts. Should a fully pregnant woman be allowed into space?! Giving birth would be even more difficult surely? Anyway, after the bomb doesn't work, they have to do something with satellites that I didn't fully understand. But it involved The Hoff leaving the shuttle to connect some wires in a satellite nearby. He's successful and this satellite sends off some laser beam that kills off all the sharks! Unfortunately he then informs his son that the shuttle doesn't have enough fuel to collect him and go back to Earth. I don't know why he couldn't go back the same way he got there but I guess he just couldn't. But before anything happens, there's sharks in space!!! Luckily Fin discovers he has a space chainsaw! Which is basically a lightsaber in the shape of a chainsaw. This comes in very handy. April manages to get eaten but Fin leaps into the shark to save her but can't find her. The shark he is inside then plummets to Earth. It's on fire but Fin manages to make a hole to the outside and fire out his parachute. He survives and escapes out of it but April is nowhere to be seen. He hears a chainsaw and it's sawing sound out of a nearby shark. A hand appears from inside the shark holding a newborn baby. April has given birth inside a shark while it fell from space! But before the film is finished a fragment of shuttle falls from the sky towards April just as the credits roll! Apparently, the fans will get to decide whether she lives or dies.

Final thoughts: When you think the Sharknado franchise can't get any crazier, it somehow does. That final sequence of events might be the most insane in any film ever. I'm not quite sure how they will top it in a fourth film. But we will find out. I don't see how anyone cannot not get some kind of enjoyment out of Sharknado 3. Whether it's from a cameo, a blood splat from a fun kill or just the craziness of it all. I love all three and Sharknado 3 might just be the best and the perfect Awfully Good film.

RABBID GRANNIES (1988)

'Grandmother, what big teeth you have!'

Synopsis: Two sweet little old ladies fall victim to an ancient curse that transforms them into bloodthirsty killers!

Director: Director Emmanuel Kervyn directed nothing else but did star in Kickboxer 2: The Road Back.

Cast: Many of the actors here either did little else exciting in the way of acting work or literally no other acting at all! The only two actors to seem to have had any career in film and TV are Elie Lison (Salamander, The Emperor of Taste) and Catherine Aymerie (The Days That Made History, Vincent).

Opening scene: Not as thrilling as usual with these but a bit odd. A priest goes into an office asking for a couple of days leave for a family party. The title appears on screen and classical music hits. As the opening credits begin to roll we see the two grannies getting out of a chauffeur driven car. They visit a town and we see them smell some cheese, give a homeless blind man some money and wine, visit a church and then the pub. And that's it.

Awfully Good character: So many to choose from here. Apart from the grannies themselves there's a host of entertaining family members who will all be mentioned below.

Awfully Good line: It's a simple one, but the priest shouting **"Holy shit!"** got a laugh out of me.

Awfully Good scene: After being shot at, one of the grannies has a pretty genius plan to stop this happening again. She comes back wearing a full medieval knights armour! The guy shoots again at her but it does no harm as she moves towards him and chops his head off with one swipe of her axe!

Other notes and scenes: I watched the dubbed version of this Belgian film, which only adds to its hilarity with the awfully done dubbing. Almost every character is unlikable and angry. It takes a while before the film gets going and we see any rabid grannies. Well they aren't actually 'rabid', they just become possessed by a demon. The initial transformation into demon grannies is a fun scene. Their (ridiculously big and over the top) birthday cake is wheeled out but no-one has a knife. Luckily, the transformation means a long knife-like nail grows from the finger of one of the grannies and she swipes down cutting the cake in two. The transformations, although cheap, do look pretty cool. Although you'd think otherwise when the housekeeper first sees the demon granny, she believes it's from "terrible indigestion". Once transformed, the 'look' of the grannies is pretty cool too. Even a bit scary and kind of Nosferatu-looking. Soon after the demons arrive people are stressing and another of my favourite lines happens. The ridiculousness of a guy shouting "Listen lesbian! Shut the hell up!". He is soon put in his place though. One granny comes flying through a painting hanging on a wall to attack a couple. Unfortunately this is badly edited, as a second later the couple are underground in the cellars trying to escape. They almost escape when they find car keys but the granny catches up with them and finds her way into the car, and is sick all over the woman. The car is stopped at this point and the demon granny starts singing happy birthday to herself. We then learn that the demons can control people. And the car is driven into a woman but she isn't run over any ordinary way. She gets stuck to the front of the car as it drives into a nearby gate, killing her off. Earlier in the film, the priest almost stabs an annoying child with a fork. This child later bites the fingers off of its mum. A fat guy gets stuck in a hole in a wall and when the demon grannies appear they rip his trousers and seem to eat from his ass! Luckily this isn't as graphic as it could have been. Finally, one of the characters gets a gun. Why he didn't get the gun earlier I'm not entirely sure. The Awfully Good scene mentioned above shows how well the gun worked. It's perhaps expected that they'd be a bit of slapstick humour but here, the 'banana skin' that is slipped on, is actually a bloody scene. I thought we might get to see the demon grannies go crazy with a gun. But they just give it to the priest to kill himself.

Final scene: This all starts with the amazing death of one guy whose body is bent backwards on itself the wrong way! Two women then hide away in a room with the grannies scratching at the door to get inside. Luckily, they have the box that the demon appeared from and it seems that destroying the box with a crucifix will make it go away. When the box is destroyed it teases that the grannies heads are going to explode. The demon head boils and moves about but then transforms back to the normal non-demon granny. Before the final credits are up, we get to hear some happy classical music while the police and ambulance arrive at the house. In the future, we see one of the survivors in a taxi and suddenly look very demon-like as a taxi driver's arm is thrown from the window!

Final thoughts: When the two demon grannies are on screen, Rabid Grannies is a fun film. It's, at times, a perfect Awfully Good film. Unfortunately they aren't on screen as much as you'd hope. And although the rest of the cast are delightfully unlikable, they're just not as entertaining as the grannies. If you think you'd like a film titled Rabid Grannies, then I can still definitely recommend this.

RED WATER (2003)

'Fear strikes, where you least expect it'

Synopsis: A group of oil workers being held hostage by a group of gangsters on a small oil rig are attacked by a freshwater bull shark.

Director: Charles Robert Carner also directed such movies as Christmas Rush, Fantasy Women Battles and an episode of Supernatural.

Cast: Lou Diamond Phillips is the main guy, John. Here's done alot of work but nothing too exciting. Maybe best known for TV shows such as Brooklyn Nine-Nine, Prodigal Son, Blue Bloods, Stargate Universe and Numb3rs. Coolio appears. Yes that Coolio. Apart from his music career, he apparently starred in a film called Pterodactyl. The original Buffy, Kristy Swanson plays the main female role. Of course, she starred in plenty else, including Flowers in the Attic, Ferris Bueller's Day Off, Dude, Where's My Car and most recently ALOT of TV movies. Principal Belding (Saved by the Bell) himself, Dennis Haskins has a small role. UK actor Langley Kirkwood appears as a tough guy. He's had roles in bigger films such as Invictus and Dredd and the show Black Sails. Gideon Emery has also appeared in Daredevil, True Blood and Teen Wolf, aswell as plenty of voice work in video games. And finally Charles Dumas hasn't had many roles but appeared in Die Hard: With a Vengeance and Deep Impact.

Opening scene: We see a grandfather and his grandson on a boat across a lake. Nearby people are blowing up things in the water, which releases a bull shark. A fisherman manages to not see the shark swim by him. Somewhere else nearby a load of teenagers are swimming and having fun when two bikini clad girls notice a shark. Everyone runs out of the water but they have to swim to a nearby anchored raft. Unfortunately, only one of them makes it. The other gets dragged under, I assume by the shark but we don't really see it. She manages to leap out of the water briefly to show us she's bleeding from the mouth but then goes back under.

Awfully Good character: This was always going to be Coolio's character 'Ice'. At one point called Ice Cube. He plays a gangster that is completely out of place in the film. Generally having no idea what is going on, so he just starts shooting at people. He is there to collect some money for his cousin that is at the bottom of the river. And he's pretty desperate to get the money even when the shark is attacking.

Awfully Good line: I was hoping Ice Cube would come up with a few but sadly he had nothing exciting to say. Instead I've gone for **"Sometimes God allows accidents to happen."** I'm not really sure what it means except to cover up bad things that happen in the world. It's from the token religious guy who says alot of similar things but then follows it up with lines like "or it could just be that the shark is hungry".

Awfully Good scene: I'm going to go with when we go back to the grandfather and grandson from the first scene. They are now fishing when grandpa's fishing rod gets pulled away and he does a very acrobatic flip into the river. Unfortunately that's the end for him. We see the water turn red and his cap floating on the surface of the water as the kid shouts "GRANDPA!". We later see the kid in a strangely amusing state of shock.

Other notes and scenes: The first thing I'm glad to report is that the actual shark actually looks pretty good most of the time. There is very little CGI used, a few shots of actual sharks and alot of shark models being used. Unfortunately, the shark is not in the movie that much. It only really gets any screen time in the last 25 minutes. The one main use of CGI sees the shark leap across a bridge to take out an unsuspecting tour guide (it would have been hard to use a real shark for that shot to be fair). Coolio does alot of attempting to look cool and tough. Usually failing at both. An oil rig starts to blow-up (the oil rig actually being the main part of the story. A shark just happens to be nearby). Panic starts with the oil rig, ending with a massive explosion, where people fly into the water, flames behind them. At one point a guy destroys a radio with his knife. I guess because that was the easiest way to do it. The old guy has to go down and turn off the oil drill underwater. The shark makes quick work of him, leaving just his arm on the wheel. Of course we get a cheesy love story. Involving exesLou Diamond Phillips and Kristy Swanson. What was almost my favourite scene involves a guy being stabbed and then casually walking across and falling off the boat. And then eaten by the shark.

Final scene: It all takes a while but a boat explodes and flames are everywhere. Coolio manages to jump off and survive. He has the money box in hand but the shark wrestles it off him. I'm not sure why the shark wanted it. Eventually the money spills out and the shark swims away while Coolio celebrates. But the shark returns and eats him head first. The two love birds manage to swim away to a ladder but the shark catches up to them. At one point, brilliantly swiping John off the ladder with its fin. It jumps at them a couple of times but they somehow avoid it. Eventually leading to a great final moment when the massive oil drill is pushed down through the sharks mouth and kills it. The happy couple now get to kiss and live happily ever after.

Final thoughts: Red Water is actually a okay enough film but there's a story here that just happens to have a shark involved on the side. The random cast are fun to watch but there's better, more fun shark films out there.

CAMEL SPIDERS (2011)

'They creep, they crawl, THEY KILL!'

Synopsis: Dozen of large, man-eating camel spiders first attack soldiers in the desert of Iraq, then invades the south western areas of the United States.

Director: Jim Wynorski has a pretty great Awfully Good CV. Including Chopping Mall, The Return of Swamp Thing, Ghoulies IV, Komodo vs Cobra, Piranhaconda, CobraGator, Attack of the 50ft Cam Girl and Giantess Battle Attack. There's some even more interesting titles like Legend of the Naked Ghost, Bigfoot or Bust and Sexually Bugged!

Cast: Actress Jon Mack has appeared in Kill Chain alongside Nicholas Cage, Saw VI, Lavalantula and its sequel, and Stormageddon! Melissa Brasselle appears in many Awfully Good movies such as Vampire In Vegas, Murderbot and The Lusty Bust Babe-a-que. One of Matthew Borlenghi's first roles was on A Nightmare on Elm Street 5: The Dream Child. Most recently he has appeared in the series Stargirl and Cobra Kai. Michael Swan starred in Dinocroc vs Supergator, Piranhaconda and Attack of the Killer Donuts! Eighties horror fans might recognise him as an officer in Friday the 13th VI: Jason Lives. Brian Krause will be best known to a lot of people as Leo Wyatt in Charmed. C. Thomas Howell's second ever film role was in E.T. and he appeared in The Amazing Spiderman. More recently he's starred in the genre series The Terror, Creepshow and The Walking Dead. Melissa Brasselle has starred in several of the director's other movies aswell as The Curse of the Komodo and Cheerleader Massacre. Frankie Cullen has appeared in the some awesomely titled films such as Monster of the Nudist Colony, Busty Coeds vs Lusty Cheerleaders and Bikini Frankenstein. Diana Terranova had a small role in Get Him to the Greek and is another who starred in Piranhaconda. She's had roles in a couple of the Sharknado movies but now seems to work with animals in movies. She was 'spider wrangler' in Knives Out and 'Insect Wrangler' in

Insidious: The Last Key. Corey Landis appeared in Dracula: Reborn and Sharkansas Women's Prison Massacre. He also played a young Red in a couple of episodes of That '70s Show. GiGi Erneta seems to play a news reporter/anchor a lot and she plays this role in Happy Death Day and its sequel Happy Death Day 2 U, and Mona Lisa and the Blood Moon. Lastly, scream queen Jessica Cameron has since starred in The Sleeper, Camp Twilight, All Through the House and Silent Night, as well as directing the horror film Truth or Dare.

Opening scene: CGI helicopters are flying above as a group of soldiers are shooting at an enemy who are shooting just as much back. Luckily for the American army, some camel spiders seem to be on their side as they kill off the enemy mid shoot out. One soldier did unfortunately die though and just before they zipped up his body bag, two spiders managed to join him. One crawling into his mouth.

Awfully Good character: Melissa Brasselle isn't entirely convincing as the bad ass Sergeant Shelly Underwood. The character is the Awfully Good stereotype tough woman that I rarely enjoy. She saves people from certain death, shoots spiders a lot and never really looks comfortable doing it.

Awfully Good line: Camel Spiders wasn't a film full of clever one-liners. This is the best it had:
"Do you know any Coldplay?"
"Is that by Hank Williams?"

Awfully Good scene: A professor and his students are searching the area when the professor notices a very big looking camel spider nearby. But he isn't scared and wants to take a closer look. He alerts the students and one mentions that it's a spider. He replies with "How many legs does it have?". One student answers with six, even though I'm certain it has 8?! Of course a few seconds later the spider jumps up and face-hugs the professor as the students flee in terror.

Other notes and scenes: Four new characters appear after the opening scene, including a woman who gets stressed very easily. She must have been having a bad day because the instant her boyfriend opened a bottle of alcohol she said she's off home and leaves in the car two minutes after arriving. Another of these characters goes to take a pee but is soon surrounded by spiders and attacked in the area that is most exposed. Like the Xenomorph's in Alien, these camel spiders enjoy a lot of face-hugging.

Even leaping from trees to do it. Two people are caught in a room full of spider webs. For some reason they look like zombies. That could have been a much different movie! We are soon told that the town this is happening in is practically dead but it seems everyone just hangs out in the local diner because that is packed. The chef in the diner lets out a beautifully high-pitched scream when he is attacked by the spiders. There are many many scenes of lots of people shooting at lots and lots of camel spiders. There is also a lot of driving around in trucks and each driving scene is made the old school way with an Awfully Good looking background in the windows of an obviously stationary car. There's a decent enough amount of blood and gore but I could have done with a little more. The spiders seem to eat peoples bodies pretty quickly. Perhaps the most frustrating thing with Camel Spiders was the side story of the four students. They survive the initial spider attack but we see them constantly running and hiding from them. The two girls (one played by Jessica Cameron) are left alone after the second guy is leapt on by a spider jumping out of the car. The face-hug I assume kills him. And from that moment we never see the girls again. I will just assume they survived and went to the drive-in cinema at the end of the film.

Final scene: Before I get to that drive in cinema, a few things happen. The Sergeant saves a little girl from a whole lot of spiders with some quick-fire shooting. She throws the girl over her shoulder but drops her gun. Her captain tells her there is no time to pick it up, despite there being plenty of time, so she runs away. They, and the remaining survivors, escape the area just in time for the Air Force to blow the place up. Everyone is happy and smiling. But lastly, we visit a drive-in. The camera moves to the back, showing the projector and then showing the sight of more spiders!

Final thoughts: Camel Spiders is quite fun in a very Awfully Good way. It's ridiculously cheesy at times and the CGI is poor but that never really matters. Maybe a sequel with giant, at least car-sized camel spiders could improve things. Oh and enough money to finish all the storylines would be good to!

LOCH NESS TERROR (2008)

'It's hunt or be hunted'

Synopsis: A rash of suspiciously gruesome murders in a sleepy lakeside town has authorities stumped. They soon realize the culprit is not only connected to the lake, but in it.

Director: Paul Ziller is quite the prolific director, with several films a year. Early in his career he directed the likes of Snakehead Terror, Android Apocalypse, Yeti, Sea Beast, Ice Quake, Ghost Storm and of course, Loch Ness Terror. But he seems to have moved on to mainly Christmas movies. He's made seven of them since 2019!

Cast: Brian Krause plays main character James Murphy. Krause hasn't done much except a whole 145 episodes of Charmed as Leo Wyatt. Since Loch Ness Terror he has starred in Poseidon Rex and the ridiculously-titled Earthtastrophe. Nial Matter has done a few TV shows including more fighting dinosaurs in Primeval: New World. He also had a part in Watchmen and 2018's The Predator. He seems to have also found a love for Christmas movies too and starred in one called Never Kiss A Man In A Christmas Sweater. Don S. Davis is another TV guy, appearing mostly in Stargate SG-1, with Loch Ness Terror being one of his last films before his death in 2008. Carrie Genzel was also in both Stargate SG-1, and Watchmen. She turned up for a couple of episodes in both Supernatural and The Walking Dead. She was also Jennifer's mum in Jennifer's Body. Amber Borycki has not done anything since 2011 but did appear in a couple of horror films such as Bloody Mary and Nightmare at the End of the Hall.

Opening scene: It's not quite as exciting or action packed as I would have liked but it does get lively eventually. Before we get to see the monster, there's a few dramatic close-ups of people and objects. Once the monster is seen emerging from the water the group decide to hand back the egg they have found. This isn't enough though as 'Nessie' walks onto land and eats one guy. Still with his legs hanging out of its mouth it swipes away another two characters, including a boy, with its neck and tail. One guy tries to escape in a car but realises the keys are with the guy Nessie is eating. Nessie spits him out and moves on to the remaining two guys but the boy survives. The CGI monster doesn't look too great in parts.

Awfully Good performance: If I'm honest, nobody was really terrible in this movie. At first, the James Murphy character threatened to be an Awfully Good and cheesy guy but turned out okay. His first scene was almost Crocodile Dundee-like. The sheriff played by Don S. Davis was amusing because of his unhelpfulness throughout. At one point suggesting Nessie's handy work was definitely down to an alligator because he'd seen it on TV.

Awfully Good line: The fact that the only one i can think of is **"Smell you later fish boy"** from the local - very un-tough looking bully - suggests this wasn't the wittiest of films.

Awfully Good scene: There are alot of fun scenes but none that really stood out, so I'm almost just picking one at random. I'm going to go for the scene where the monster is heard by a woman. She retreats to her car and watches on as Nessie walks through the forest in front of her, as high as the trees, looking like a Diplodocus. It then rips off the car door and as we see the remains later, kills the woman.

Other notes and scenes: One of the first deaths is an old guy who knows Nessie is real and is desperate to prove it to everyone else who just thinks he is crazy. He sets up a camera and just when he's ready to snap, Nessie splashes water over him and rises out of the water biting both of his arms off. With blood spurting out of his stumps, he gets eaten in one quick mouthful. Nessie of course gets to eat a few fisherman. The CGI ranges from the usual and okay, to pretty damn bad. One of the worst CGI moments is unfortunately in what could of been one of the better death scenes, as a girl gets her head bitten off. The most annoying character (the aforementioned 'bully') appears in one of the worst looking but thankfully short 'fight' scenes ever. Luckily he meets his maker when he just ignores the proven advice that standing still means the monsters (Nessie and its babies) won't be able to see you. He attempts to run away but gets eaten by several mini monsters. The Sheriff gets pushed off a cliff by the babies and then eaten. While one of the most horrific looking scenes was actually the babies eating dead bodies. One main character thinks hiding in a hollow tree trunk was the best thing to do against Nessie. It didn't really work. Nessie does, like many monsters in these films do, seem to be able to sneak up on people. Shallow water is still no match for a sneaky giant sea monster.

Final scene: There's actually a whole lot going on in the final moments. Lot of gadgets and guns don't seem to be working, including some strange gun that fired waves of some sort (micro-waves?!) that burnt Nessie a bit. It ended up coming down to an almost comedic giant needle that Nessie needed to be injected with. Of course it wasn't that simple, the monster swiped it out of Murphy's hand at first. But lots of dramatic close-ups later and he had it back, injecting into Nessie and then setting her on fire. One big CGI explosion later and Nessie and her babies (who luckily were in the general area too) were dead. Everything is capped off with a kiss by the two main younger characters. The girl seemingly not that bothered that her boyfriend died just minutes before.

Final thoughts: Loch Ness Terror, which by the way is set in Canada, the monster made it there it seems, is actually very watchable but never really gets that good. It's nowhere near the worst Awfully Good film I've watched and there's plenty of fun to be had.

ANACONDAS: TRAIL OF BLOOD (2009)

'Bigger, faster, hungrier'

Synopsis: A genetically created Anaconda, cut in half, regenerates itself into two aggressive giant snakes, due to the Blood Orchid.

Director: Don E. FauntLeRoy (that's quite the name) took on this fourth Anacondas film after previously directing number three (Offspring). He clearly had a spell of enjoying making Awfully Good movies because he also directed Damn Sea Vampires! And Snakehead Swamp. He would perhaps prefer to be remembered for his cinematography work on Cobra Kai and many more movies.

Cast: Crystal Allen appeared in the third film of the series , Anaconda: The Offspring. Linden Ashby has appeared in a few horror related media, including Resident Evil: Extinction and the recent Teen Wolf TV series and movie. He also played Johnny Cage in the 1995 Mortal Kombat movie. Danny Midwinter has featured in many UK TV shows including Dream Team and Eastenders, aswell as the Johnny Depp horror, From Hell. John Rhys-Davies is best known for his roles in the Indiana Jones and Lord of the Rings films. Dan Badarau has appeared in horror films with great titles such as Teenage Space Vampires and Werewolf: The Beast Among Us. Ana Ularu has gone on to have roles in Siberia, the Alex Rider series and Tom Clancy's Jack Ryan.

Opening scene: We have a guy narrating himself as he is working in some kind of animal laboratory, playing around with test tubes. He leaves the place as we see a big CGI snake in a cage. The snake attempts to escape while the other animals go crazy. And then it actually escapes, finds the guy and attacks him, we assume eating him.

Awfully Good character: Has to be the British guy. Unfortunately all the characters are much of nothing, with accents being one of the only differences. But this guy at least overreacts to things beautifully. He gets angry and emotional very quickly. And eventually needlessly sacrifices himself to the snake to save someone else.

Awfully Good line: Sadly, there's nothing. The longer the film went on the more I tried to find one. But this film was way too serious and cheesy for any great lines.

Awfully Good scene: It's only a short moment but one guy sacrifices himself, again seemingly for no real reason. He runs directly at the snake firing a tiny gun that has little to no effect. Once the bullets run out he just kind of stands there and the snake grabs him and swings him about in the air for a while before eating him. The shot of the snake doing this is from a distance and looks pretty good. By far the best shot in the film.

Other notes and scenes: One of the first dramatic moments with the snake is when a woman is running away from it and she shoots at it but of course it has no effect. Luckily just as it is just about to attack, the ceiling above it collapses and seemingly kills the snake. But this snake doesn't die that easy. After escaping that, the woman falls about
three foot off of a ladder and somehow knocks herself out. Here she has memories of a previous snake attack, which I assume are from this films prequel(s).
The snake, at times, seems pretty slow when chasing people on the run but as soon as it's chasing a car, it manages to keep up with the pace. I'm also sure the size of the snake changes throughout the film. Maybe this explains the speed problem. Some of the characters make some awful decisions. Such as deciding it was better to leave the safety of house to run through the forest that the snake is in. Or when in the house to take a pee outside in the dark where the snake is waiting nearby. There is a story about a old guy dying of cancer who sends five 'assassins' to get the serum and kill the people involved in making it. At one point the five guys are running away from the snake when one of them trips. He is mocked for this trip and responds by shooting the guy in the leg that mocked him! There's another great fall moment when a girl falls but we see it in beautiful slow motion. One guy decides if he is going to die, he might aswell take the snake with him. He has a grenade pulled and ready to

blow. But the snake just turns the other way. The snake does get blown to bits more than once but the serum it has been filled with means it can re-animate. Oh, the serum by the way can apparently make you live forever. One guy gets shot about 100 times in one brief moment. The old guy eventually gets the serum but while celebrating this the snake appears, wraps itself around him and bites his head off.

Final scene: I actually almost forgot there was a snake involved at this point. This strangely starts as a chase scene. A pretty decent one to be fair. The bad guy manages to leap on the back of the Jeep that the other characters are trying to escape on. There's some fighting while two guys hang off the back of the Jeep until eventually the bad guy is kicked off and nicely lands in the snakes mouth. However, he had explosives on him which then explode and the snake again is in pieces. But, as the surviving characters drive away, we of course discover that the anaconda is still alive!

Final thoughts: Anacondas: Trail of Blood just took itself way too seriously and wasn't that much fun at all. Poor CGI and an awful story don't help much either.

GRABBERS (2012)

*'In 1759 Ireland invented the pint.
In 2012 it'll save their lives.'*

Synopsis: When an island off the coast of Ireland is invaded by bloodsucking aliens, the heroes discover that getting drunk is the only way to survive.

Director: Jon Wright seems to have settled down with episodes of very normal TV shows but between 2009 and 2014 he made the teen revenge horror Tormented, Grabbers and Robot Overlords.

Cast: Lead actor Richard Coyle has been acting over 25 years now, with his biggest roles in Prince of Persia: Sands of Time and more recently Fantastic Beasts: The Secret of Dumbledore and as Father Faustus Blackwood in hit Netflix show The Chilling Adventures of Sabrina. The lead female is played by Ruth Bradley. Best known to me for her part in the TV show Primeval but more recently starring in the fantastic Ted Lasso. Russel Tovey is very recognisable to anyone who watches TV in Britain. Horror fans will probably know him from Being Human but he also recently popped up in American Horror Story. Horror fans will also know Lalor Roddy from the film Boy Eats Girl and recent show Wreck. David Pearse has appeared in the TV show Vikings, aswell as The Guard, Fifty Dead Men Walking, The Banshees of Inisherin and Let The Wrong One In. Bronagh Gallagher has appeared in some huge films including Pulp Fiction, Star Wars: Episode One - The Phantom Menace and Sherlock Holmes. Michael Hough has starred in Boys From County Hell and played a Hobgoblin the very funny TV show What We Do In The Shadows.

Opening scene: A boat is out at sea as, what looks like, a meteor flies pass and lands nearby. The three men on board go to investigate. One of them quickly disappears off screen and overboard. The next is hooked away quickly via some tentacle and taken overboard. The last one, I assume dies as the camera goes point of view as the monster goes towards him.

Awfully Good character: No-one stuck out too much but I'm going to go with two characters. Paddy and Brian. Paddy is the local drunk fisherman and is played by Lalor Roddy. Brian is the local bar owner played by David Pearse. They have a fun back and forth throughout the film. Paddy says "feck off" a lot, which is way more amusing than it should be. Brian tries to be a hero at one point with his water pistol full of petrol, but that soon fails. Soon after, him and Paddy are fighting each other. It doesn't last long and no-one connects with the other as they are both very drunk.

Awfully Good line: There was a few funny back and fourths but I liked this one the most. When several characters are discussing weapons they have, someone declares they have a pellet gun.
"What are you gonna do with a pellet gun?
Shoot pellets.....but i don't have any pellets."

Awfully Good scene: This is less a scene and more of a moment. But Brian holding his water pistol like he is The Terminator, ready for action (but very drunk) holds the pistol out for Adam (Tovey) to light the end of it. The only problem is, that Adam is on the floor and also very drunk. It takes a long time for him to crawl and light the pistol. When it's all done Brian runs out at the giant grabber firing away. Only it's raining a lot and the light goes out very quickly, leaving him just firing petrol at the thing.

Other notes and scenes: Drunk people has featured heavily in the scenes above and the reason many people are drunk in this film is that the grabbers are kind of 'allergic' to alcohol. They drink blood but if the blood is full of alcohol they won't eat the people. So obviously everybody needs to get drunk!
I liked one of the early lines that "It's always the quiet places where the mad shit happens". There's a quick glimpse of the original Night of the Living Dead on somebodies TV early on. The first look at any grabber is only a small one. And it looks like a blue octopus. The first proper attack they do, is a face hug just like the face-huggers in Alien. I liked that this being set in Ireland and not say, America, as the characters don't have guns. They have to make do with a nail gun, water pistols.....a piece of wood with a nail in it. That kind of thing. The nail gun appears in an amusing moment as Lisa (Bradley) drunkenly fires it narrowly past someone's face. The CGI for the grabbers is actually pretty great

throughout and not in an Awfully Good way. Adam doesn't get eaten by a grabber but does get flung many miles away by it's tentacle.

Final scene: It is quite drawn out but it's a lot of fun. The two main characters Ciaran and Lisa drunkenly drive away from the giant grabber. It swiftly follows them to a nearby area. They split up when they arrive there. Lisa goes to look for a crane with a grabber of its own and Ciaran, well, runs to safety I think. He has to stumble across a bridge that is falling apart and then destroyed by the grabber. He thinks he can goad the grabber to nearby tanks which he will blow up. But the grabber is having none of it and uses it's tongue to knock him off the roof he is on. Just when it looks like he'll be gone, Lisa arrives with a digger! She rams into the grabber while falling with the digger down a slope, crushing it underneath the digger. The two then start to celebrate, when a tentacle comes out of nowhere and grabs Ciaran. Luckily he has Paddy's homebrew with him and pours it in the grabbers mouth. Lisa then fires a flare gun at it, leading to a big explosion!

Of course, by the final moment we discover there are still some grabber eggs left!

Final thoughts: Grabbers is a decent little film. Not quite as Awfully Good as I thought it would be. But that's not to say it takes itself too seriously. There's plenty to enjoy here. Grab a few beers before watching and you'll love it!

RAIDERS OF THE LOST SHARK (2015)

'Even Indiana Jones can't get out of this one!'

Synopsis: A prehistoric shark is released into the waters near a small lake community as a result of an oil drilling accident, and proceeds to wreak havoc on nearby swimmers.

Director: Scott Patrick's film before this was Rise of the Black Bat. He has gone on to make plenty of Awfully Good movies, usually with pun-heavy titles, including Countrycide, Ouija Shark, Konga TNT and Heavy Metal Werewolf.

Cast: Peter Whittaker hasn't had a long career but he's featured in Homicycle, My Fair Zombie and Hell At My Heels. Him and the director clearly get along well because he has featured in several of his films, including Konga TNT, Ouija Shark and Tis the Season. Pavel Lubanski also starred in Homicycle and another Scott Patrick film - Galaxy warriors. Add another few for Patrick's Homicycle (about a vigilante on a motorcycle, not just a normal cycle like I hoped) with Candice Lidstone, Catherine Mary Clark, Mel Guibz and Anik Rompre. Ian Quick was also in Homicycle but had experience with sharks after
appearing in Attack of the Jurassic Shark! Scott McClelland also starred in Wolf Girl and Zombie Beach Party. A lot of the cast also seem to have appeared in a film called Biff Wellington. Jessica Huether starred in Unholy Night, which has now be added in my 'to watch' Christmas movie list. John Migliore starred in, what I'm sure was great follow-up, Ouija Shark 2.

Opening scene: Well there's not much of one to write about. There's some opening credits explaining this is a true story but ending with 'just messing'. Then we get two cops who get with two women while on shift. After some awful dialogue they decided to go to a nearby lake, where we see some close-ups of a terrible looking CGI sharks mouth. Most of the opening cast soon get eaten, well they disappear underwater and don't appear again. The very cheap looking opening credits then role with some equally awful music. The credits show a band called Fatal Mistake are used for the music. Too many jokes....

Awfully Good character: Captain Stuben played by Scott McClelland. The character seems to be based on the sea captain in The Simpsons. And at least the actor is having some fun with it. Like most of the film it's much more miss than hit but he gets a couple of laughs.

Awfully Good line: There's a few awful lines but my favourite was probably *"Come on out.....you......flying fish!"*. Yep, the shark do fly.

Awfully Good scene: If I'm honest there's not a whole lot. The scene when several students get uneventfully eaten comes to mind. Mainly because after the shark eats a couple of them, one of the remaining women decides to phone her professor to ask what to do. Just stay on the boat surely?! She doesn't manage that but does manage to stay on the phone while in the sea and it keeps working. The advice the professor gives does actually work too.

Other notes and scenes: There are two characters in the film called 'Spaz' and 'Weiner'. Thankfully we never see them and they are just there for poor attempts at humour. The CGI in Raiders of the Lost Shark might be some of the worst I have ever seen. The shark attacks people in the water but leaves no ripple effect on the water and the shark disappears instantly in shallow water. The 'flying' sharks consist of a badly drawn shark quickly moving across and taking up the whole of the screen. It's hilariously bad. Luckily the characters can just duck out of the way if they fly towards them. Oh, and the title, despite its greatness, means absolutely nothing in connection with the actual storyline. Not quite as entertaining as the captain is, 'crazy shark owner guy'. He's not as crazy as he tries to be. Even when holding a gun he doesn't come across as a threat.

Final scene: Like the opening scene, there's not much of one. Crazy guy loses his gun in the most poorly executed 'twist' you'll ever see. Leaving the two surviving women (the professor and student) to kill the one flying shark. They have one small gun and a small explosive. They throw the explosive towards the flying shark who nicely eats it and explodes in one quick motion. The one bit of blood then splashes over a cop.

Final thoughts: This somehow runs for about one hour. The film-makers couldn't entertain us any longer. It might be the worst film I've ever seen but I kind of like it. That's a lie, I do like it. It is Awfully Good and although it's sometimes unwatchable, it's somehow completely entertaining in the worst way. You might just love it, and hate it.

ARACHNOQUAKE (2012)

'The world will quiver in fear'

Synopsis: An earthquake triggers a brood of giant fire-breathing spiders to attack the city of New Orleans.

Director: Griff Furst is well known to Awfully Good fans. He's also directed Ghost Shark, Swamp Shark, Nightmare Shark, Shark Shock and Lake Placid 3. Unfortunately he hasn't directed anything since 2018 and is now better known for his acting, including several episodes of the excellent Banshee and the Will Smith starring Focus.

Cast: Megan Adelle appeared in the Straw Dogs remake a year before this but has only starred in 2017's Portrait of an American Family since Arachnoquake. Gralen Bryant Banks has appeared in Pitch Perfect 2, the Oldboy remake, Green Book and Queen & Slim. Paul Boocock is best known for his voice work on Adult Swim animated show The Venture Bros. Bug Hall appeared in the film I never knew existed, the sequel Honey, We Shrunk Ourselves. He did well in the nineties, also appearing in Little Rascals and The Stupids. Through his song in Little Rascals - 'You Are So Beautiful', he also gets a credit on the soundtrack for Baby Driver. Grant James has featured in things as diverse as Tombstone and Dumb and Dumber To. Lucky Johnson starred in Ghost Shark and episodes of True Detective, Treme and American Horror Story. Earl Maddox has starred in the Awfully Good film Monsterwolf as well as Abraham Lincoln: Vampire Hunter but has worked in very little since Arachnoquake. Ethan Phillips appeared in the best Purge movie 'Election Year' and a couple of episodes of Better Call Saul. Tracey Gold is known for playing Carol Seaver in the long-running show Growing Pains. Ned Yousef has been popping up in lots of cool stuff lately, including Bill and Ted Face the Music, Ms Marvel and We Have A Ghost. And finally, most people will know Edward Furlong. Even if not by name you would have seen him as John Connor in Terminator 2: Judgment Day and Danny in American History X.

Opening scene: There's a few people packing eggs outside talking about an Earthquake the night before. A small weird looking CGI spider crawls into an egg box as a guy goes looking for whatever killed a couple of chickens the night before. He discovers a big hole in the road. Before he investigates properly he checks out his 'bite' mark on his shoulder. What we see is a big cyst which then explodes and a spider leaps out. The spider then chases the man to the hole, which he falls down followed by the spider.

Awfully Good character: Bug Hall as Paul, the hero of the film. He's not particularly exciting and he's your typical Awfully Good hero. He starts off as the womanising drunk, whose Father is ready to disown but after not caring about anybody except himself for most the film, ends up killing the spiders, saving the day and being loved by everyone.

Awfully Good line: There were actually quite a few to choose from. But the character Jean Jacques wins this for his line towards the end of the film aimed at the Queen spider, *"Time to dance you big beautiful bitch!"*

Awfully Good scene: At some point during the film we discover the spiders, well at least some of the spiders, can breath fire! With this, one of them attacks Edward Furlong and his female team of baseball players. Luckily, one of those players doesn't hide and scream in the bus like all the others. This one keeps hold of a baseball bat and when Furlong's character kicks the giant spider towards her she swings and hits it home run-style as it lands with an explosion.

Other notes and scenes: As well as baseball bats, an old guy uses his walking stick like a golf club to bat off some spiders. The spiders range from 'normal' size to almost human size and right up to the Queen spider size which is as big as a house and can climb skyscrapers. Fire first comes into play when two characters use aerosols and lighters to kill a few of the smaller spiders. As well as fire breathing skills, the spiders have another trick up their sleeve. They can also walk on water! Well actually, run as fast as boats on water. The writer clearly wanted to be relevant with current environmental issues because fracking is blamed for the spiders at one point. There's one nice slow motion on fire death but the death scenes unfortunately aren't entertaining or gory enough.

Final scene: The Queen spider is high up the side of a skyscraper and the army are struggling to deal with it. One group of them just get set on fire relatively easily. Luckily, our group of heroes have a plan. It's a ridiculous one but it's a plan. Paul gets into some kind of underwater outfit and plans on getting inside the spider and blowing it up via the gas part of its stomach that it uses for the fire breathing. With this, we get some action hero music and Jean Jacques manages to steal a bazooka from the army. And despite not looking in great shape he runs off with it with the army in chase but unable to stop him. And when he does use it, it doesn't do a whole lot. Jean Jacques is killed by the spider but soon after Paul is inside. He gets 'pooed' out which means he can then blow up the spider and somehow survive. Upon the Queen spider dying, so do all the other spiders, like some weird sci-fi film where all the robots are connected.

Final thoughts: Arachnoquake is actually pretty entertaining and the acting is a small step-up from the usual Awfully Good films. True horror fans will be disappointed with the gore (or lack of it) but with director Griff Furst you know what you're getting and it's usually fun.

PIRANHACONDA (2012)

'Half fish, half snake…All death'

Synopsis: Piranha/anaconda hybrid creatures hunt down the scientist who stole their egg, as well as a film crew making a slasher film in the jungle.

Director: Jim Wynorski is quite the prolific director with a IMDb that includes 107 credits as director! His second ever movie came in 1986 and it's the excellent cult classic Chopping Mall. Notable movies since then include The Return of Swamp Thing, Sorority House Massacre II, Ghoulies IV, Komodo vs Cobra and the quadrilogy (?!) of The Bare Wench Project films. Still making films in 2023, he could easily have his own book of Awfully Good movies.

Cast: Michael Madsen is still quite popular but will seemingly act in anything. Once you've featured in Celebrity Big Brother, I feel like your acting career probably isn't going so well. But in 2023 here's still featuring in a number of movies. It will be no surprise to anyone that his last good performances have been in Tarantino film's (although I'd argue he wasn't great in Once Upon Time In Hollywood or The Hateful Eight). He actually puts in a decent performance here which is the most shocking thing. Maybe he enjoys this type of movie because he's also starred in Megalodon, Cobragator and Shark Attack. Rachel Hunter also appears. Outside of her modelling, she is perhaps best known for once being married to Rod Stewart. And maybe being 'Stacey's Mom' in the Fountains of Wayne music video. Here, she looked unconvincing holding a gun. Rib Hillis (what kind of name is Rib?!) has also featured in Dinocroc vs Supergator, Psycho Storm Chaser and Sharktopus vs Pteracuda! Between Awfully Good movies and straight to daytime movies he seems to find regular work. And Chris De Christopher I'm mentioning just because of his name. But he has starred in a film called Wolf Man vs Piranha Man: Howl of the Piranha, Sharkansas Women's Proison Massacre, Attack of the

Killer Donuts and the amazingly titled The Devil Wears Nada. So maybe he should have got a bigger role here.

Opening scene: As is normally the case, the action was plentiful in the opening scene. First, I have to mention the music. It is indeed awfully good, it's a bad pop song made for the film, with a chorus of 'Piranhaconda' sang loudly. Please check it out on Youtube. Now, back to the scene. We see Michael Madsen with some other explorers and soon the Piranhaconda has noticed them, leaping out of a lake to eat one of them in one quick swoop. Just before this happens Madsen has got one of its eggs. He seems to know alot about them somehow. The Piranhaconda then chases down and eats a girl before taking out the helicopter that was going to take them back. While this all happens Madsen remains calm and looks cool.

Awfully Good performance: It has to be Rachel Hunter. She looks even more uncomfortable shooting a gun than she did holding it. Despite this she does get to be involved in one of the best lines....

Awfully Good line: As promised, Rachel Hunter is involved.
"Something much worse. It's like a unholy union between a piranha and an anaconda.
 You mean a piranhaconda?
 I can't believe you just said that."

Awfully Good scene: When the piranhaconda swoops down and takes out - eats or bites in half - three, yes three, people in a second! It might have been over very quickly but it was great!

Other notes and scenes: Some of the people in the nearby jungle are there filming a slasher film, Head Chopper I believe it's called. So that brings up a few awfully good scenes itself of people screaming a lot and being chased by a very unscary killer. Maybe they should make that film.
There's a few other notable lines. "Suck lead you hillbilly butt nugget!", "That loco chica, she played kickball with my cojones", and "I hate bad news" (cos other people love bad news right?), were my favourites. They even managed to get an Anchorman quote in there with "I'm kind of a big deal around here". Most of the deaths, and there's alot of them, feature a brief explosion of blood and are over in a couple of seconds. The piranhaconda is surprisingly stealth like too. For something so big it sneaks up on people very often. Oh and it roars, I'm not sure why

or how.

Final scene: The final scene is awfully good. The two survivors are on top of a waterfall with the piranhaconda staring them down. They throw the egg at it (this is how it was following them, so obviously they kept it) but the egg also has explosives around it. Piranhaconda catches it in its mouth and the two survivors leap into the water below (again, I'm not sure why this was necessary) and pressed the detonator, blowing it's head off. As they get out of the water they share a kiss, only to be eaten by a second piranhaconda that I think may have been mentioned at one point.

Final thoughts: Despite a high death count, Piranhaconda wasn't that entertaining. Michael Madsen was always looking cool but the rest of the cast were pretty awful. Although I still wouldn't be opposed to a more action filled sequel!

LAKE PLACID 2 (2007)

'One giant crocodile in the lake was a problem. THREE giant crocodiles are going to be a nightmare'

Synopsis: Man-eating crocodiles return to the lake, as two males and one aggressive female crocodile protecting their nest, wreak havoc on the locals.

Director: David Flores hasn't exactly had a prolific directorial career and hasn't made anything since The Exterminators in 2013. What got him the Lake Placid sequel job was probably his first movie Boa Vs. Python.

Cast: John Scneider who starred as Bo Duke in Dukes of Hazard and I thought here, looked alot like Sam Trammell of True Blood fame. He also played Jonathan Kent for 114 episodes of Smallville but I wont pretend to know anything about that superhero show. Sarah Lafleur has done lots of TV including sixteen episodes of Ugly Betty. Maybe more notably she has done voice work for several Sailor Moon projects aswell as voice work in the video games Devil May Cry and Viewtiful Joe: Battle Carnival. Sam McMurray is recognisable from lots if stuff, for me as Chandler's boss in Friends. He recently did some voice work in the excellent Netflix animated Christmas movie Klaus. Chad Michael Collins has starred in Rock Monster and Legion of the Dead. And is also someone who does a bit of voice acting including a couple of Call of Duty video games. He also appeared an episode of the Shudder series Creepshow. Alicia Ziegler hasn't done a whole lot but did appear in a film called Wolf Town. And Joe Holt appeared in the fun horror film Blood Shot. Cloris Leachman sadly died in 2021 and was best known for her role in Young Frankenstein. Towards the end of her career she was still putting in great performances as the gran in The Croods movies.

Opening scene: It is short and sweet but involves a guy getting his arm bitten off, blood flowing everywhere, with actually good, non CGI, effects.

Awfully Good performance: No-one was terrible in this film. But to be honest no-one is great either! So I'll go with Sam McMurray. For no other reason than in my head he will always be Chandler's Boss. So I kinda of had that character in my mind whenever he popped up on screen.

Awfully Good Line: This exchange got a proper chuckle out of me. Delivered perfectly.
A: Struther's a pretty good pilot?
B: No, not really.
  He's failed every flight test known to man.
  He's crashed three times already.
  Once was even into an elementary school.
  Poor kids.
  Basically, he's the last person on the Earth who should be flying a plane.
A: What?
B: It was nothing.

Other notes and scenes: There's alot of scenes with women in their underwear, I'm sure plenty of genre fans will be pleased with that. There's even some slow motion nudity. An early scene involves several people setting bait for the crocodile and then hiding close by behind a bush. Once they have the bait they swing it in its net only for the (very CGI'ed) crocodile to gulp it down! In this scene and several others, some of the characters don't seem that scared of these giant crocodiles. One scene sees a nice tug of war with a girl as the rope. Unsurprisingly the crocodile wins and the girls loses limbs. The three crocodiles we discover are named Max, George Jr and Martha. Each crocodile varies in size and I don't mean with each other. I mean the same crocodile seems to change in size in different scenes. An Awfully Good movie trait now.
One character falls out of a tree while sleeping and lands on a crocodile. Obviously he doesn't notice but everyone makes a lot of noise when his friends tell him. There's plenty of limbs lost throughout, one death sees a head bitten off and spat out.

Final scene: It's all a bit of a let down really. The crocs are killed off relatively easily and we get a cheesy ending. The two survivors start passionately kissing. I mean why not, crocodile killing is passionate stuff. And then to add to it all, the dog that earlier looked like it had been eaten, returns alive and well! All making one seriously happy ending.

Final thoughts: Lake Placid 2 is a bit of a let down. Even for my low Awfully Good standards. The first Lake Placid was fun (and I didn't think awful enough to feature in this collection, this sequel has its moments but really is not half as much fun as it should be.

SHARK ATTACK (1999)

'There's blood in the water'

Synopsis: In a once serene African fishing village, a marine biologist goes in search of some answers when his friend becomes a victim in one of a series of brutal shark attacks.

Director: Director Bob Misiorowski has seven films to his name and at the age of 71 (he was almost 50 when his first movie - Blink of an Eye - was released) while he had his last film, Hardin, released in 2015.

Cast: Ernie Hudson was of course Winston in the Ghostbusters movies. He's also starred in cult classic The Crow and the recent reboot of Quantum Leap. Casper Van Dien will always be best known for his star role in Starship Troopers but in the same year Shark Attack was released he starred in Sleepy Hollow. He's also appeared in Alita: Battle Angel, Sharktopus Vs. Whalewolf (I need to see that one!) and Christmas Twister. Cordeel McQueen doesn't do much acting work and is more of a stunts and special effects guy. Working on films such as Resident Evil: The Final Chapter, Doomsday,The Woman King and Maze Runner: The Death Cure. Chris Olley has appeared in American Ninja 4 and Tarzan and the Lost City. Jenny McShane appeared in an episode of Grimm and returned for Shark Attack 3: Megalodon. Recently she has worked as a visual effects producer in shows such as This Is Us and Only Murders In the Building. And finally, Lee-Anne Liebenberg (who plays 'Woman in the Bikini here) starred in Death Race 2 and Doomsday but has also done stunt work in Bloodshot, I Am Not A Witch and Avengers: Age of Ultron.

Opening scene: We are in Africa of all places. A guy is scuba diving, but before we see any shark he is back on a boat. We see a close-up of him changing his watch, which seems really odd but later on we discover this is (almost) important. All of a sudden, while working on his computer, he is attacked from behind and the opening title appears.

Awfully Good character: No exciting or strange characters in Shark Attack. But the two police officers did amuse me. Always trying to look tough, and despite occasionally killing people, never actually looking very tough. They're also in most of the exciting scenes in the film.

Awfully Good line: It's short and sweet but Van Dien's character saying *"Holy cow"*, amused me no end. Does anyone really say that? Even in 1999.

Awfully Good scene: A woman is relaxing on the side of a boat, casually just dangling one leg over the side. A leg that I'm sure looks tasty for any passing shark. And sure enough a shark gets her leg and pulls her in. The water becomes red as Casper stabs the shark with a harpoon. The woman survives but there's not much of her leg left.

Other notes and scenes: The first scene continues after the opening title, with the guy having his arm cut with a machete by a police officer. His blood drips into the water as he is thrown in and fed to the shark. We see a shark open his mouth and the guy going deeper in the water but they're not on screen at the same time. A lot of the shark footage is actually real sharks just swimming about in some water. I assume it's probably just stock footage of sharks. One of the many reasons sharks are bad, is obviously that they effect tourism (Just ask the mayor in Jaws). Casper is involved in almost every scene. Early on he gets in a western-like bar fight with some locals, only to moments later bond with a guy he was fighting when they both save a boy from a shark who fell out of his boat. The shark was nearby but I can't say I felt much tension as it approached. A shark manages to get on to the boat at one point, causing major panic. I'm not sure why really. Surely that's the one place you'd fancy your chances versus a shark! Like many of these films, there seems to be lots of work going on in labs. The reason here is that they are testing steroids on sharks that can cure cancer. Trouble is, it gives the sharks enlarged brains and makes them constantly hungry (I mean if it means curing cancer I guess we'll take it). One scene sees the shark attack two characters while they are in one of them underwater metal cages. They worry and panic again but for no real reason. They're in a solid metal cage. The camera shakes around a lot though, so you can sense their panic. There is one big car chase, where the two police officers continuously shoot aimlessly. It all ends when one police car crashes and instantly explodes. Aswell as a car chase, we get a boat race! It's much the same as the car chase but on water. The cops shoot a bit more accurately but get upended when Casper creates a makeshift bomb and throws it at them. But his boat also ends up in flames after another big explosion.

Final scene: The villain explains his plan to the good guys and then goes about trying to kill them. But before he gets the chance there's another big explosion. We're surrounded by water so there's lots of gun shots and lots of people falling into water from great heights. Infact, I'd pretty much forgotten this film had sharks in it at one point. Luckily it's not all aimless shooting, one police officer attempts to keep using his machete and the sometimes bad sometimes good scientist gets shot with a harpoon. It finally comes down to Casper and the main villain. Casper jumps on to the helicopter he is escaping from and fights him while dangling out of the side of it. He eventually gets in and throws the bad guy out of the helicopter and into the water. But for some reason, Casper jumps in and follows him. The helicopter then crashes and explodes. Obviously. With Casper and the villain in the water we are then reminded that there are still sharks in the movie. At first a shark just swims past casually, not really bothering with the two humans fighting nearby. But eventually the shark must have got hungry or something because he eats the bad guy. The final moments see Casper and his new girlfriend kiss and leave on a boat.

Final thoughts: Shark Attack is pretty much exactly how you'd expect it to be. Not over the top or ridiculous enough to be that entertaining but it's actually quite watchable.

MONSTRO! (2010)

*'The were told to never go into the water,
now the sea will rise in a sea of blood'*

Synopsis: Three killer vixens hang-out at a seaside cabin and in the meantime have to do battle with a the locals and a deadly creature from the deep.

Director: Stuart Simpson has since directed Chocolate Strawberry Vanilla. A comedy about an ice cream van man and the segment 'M is for Mutant' in ABCs of Death 2.5.

Cast: This is an Australian film, so obviously at least one cast member has appeared in Neighbours. Kyrie Capri is the lucky actor this time. Norman Yemm also appeared in Neighbours, as well as Prisoner Cellblock H and another sea-based series, Moby Dick. Several of the actors here have only appeared in this film and nothing else. You can add Scott Brennan to the list of actors who starred in Neighbours. David Gannon hasn't appeared in a whole lot but did turn up in last year's Elvis.

Opening scene: It's kind of long but interesting. Some old music is playing and the picture is black and white as we see three women with their broken down car. Another car arrives with two guys who can't believe their luck. The girls pull there best sexy poses as the guys pull over and try to help them with the car. Unfortunately for the two men, these women aren't who they seem and the first guy has his throat slit inside the car as the blood spurts all over the windscreen. As his friend sees this, his throat is cut and blood spurts all over the bonnet. The women start to clean up the mess and drag the bodies away.

Awfully Good character: Snowball. Pretty much just because she is called Snowball.

Awfully Good line: There's a few pretty bad ones but a father and son chat

on a fishing trip brings up the best one.
*"**Women are all the same son. Sluts. Just like your mother!**"* Charming.

Awfully Good scene: Probably the last scene but I'll mention that later. So the first scene we see the sea beast will have to get this honour. A fishing boat is attacked by its tentacles. Well I'm sure the whole beast attacked it but we only see the tentacles. A hand is ripped off, bodies get dragged away, heads are sucked and blood squirts everywhere! All with no sound, just the score and all with practical effects.

Other notes and scenes: There's quite a lot of girls in bikinis scenes. But strangely no-one is ever attacked while they're actually in the sea. I mentioned some bad lines earlier. This is a film that has characters say such things as "by Jeeves!" and "relax toots. We're amigos now". The tentacles attack and kill the already mentioned father and son. They aim for the neck this time but the result, and blood, is the same. There's a fun moment just before the end when one of the women decides that's it, she'll run out the cabin she's in and kill the monster herself with a single knife. She runs out the door but the camera stays on the door. A few seconds later the door flies open as the woman runs back in screaming.

Final scene: From there, the cabin starts shaking and everything starts happening. The octopus-looking monster surrounds and kind of engulfs the cabin, attempting to kill the people inside with its tentacles. It again goes for peoples necks and faces but is stabbed a few times. We then see its giant eye looking in as well as its mouth. A pitch fork is found to do some damage to the tentacles but the two women fighting it are struggling. So the 17 year old girl who has been hiding in the room below with her grandfather, decides to help. She brings a shotgun but can't help Snowball as she dies. Blood is everywhere as Snowball has her head sucked clean off for a decapitation. And her head is thrown to one side. But the other women throws the fork at it's eye and the 17 year old shoots in it's mouth which is enough for it to wander off. For now at least. Or until a sequel happens.

Final thoughts: Monstro! is very much a film of two scenes. The first and last ones. It does have a few entertaining moments in between but it needed more monster action and probably a little more humour too. The final 15 minutes or so though are extremely fun and exactly how I'd want this whole movie to be like.

MEGALODON (2002)

'60 feet of prehistoric terror'

Synopsis: A deep-sea drilling operation goes horribly wrong, releasing the deadliest ocean predator that has ever roamed the seas since prehistoric times-Carcharodon Megalodon...sixty feet of prehistoric terror.

Director: Pat Corbitt only directed one other movie but its title makes it worthwhile alone. That title you ask? Are you ready for this? - How The Hamsters Saved Winter.

Cast: Robin Sachs is a face most will recognise. He did a lot of voice acting but also appeared in Buffy the Vampire Slayer, Galaxy Quest and The Lost World: Jurassic Park. Al Sapienza has been seen in Godzilla and the TV show, Gotham. This year he appeared in Big George Foreman. Mark Sheppard is best known for his role as Crowley in Supernatural. His other TV roles include Doom Patrol, Warehouse 13 and Doctor Who. Evan Mirand has had big gaps in his career but has appeared in Fight Club and Se7en. Gary J. Tunnicliffe is usually a special effects and make-up artist but has appeared as an actor in two Dracula films, a Halloween film, a Hellraiser film, Dinoshark and Feast!

Opening scene: Megalodon might have one of the least interesting opening scenes for a film of its type. We watch a documentary news show called 'Quest' which has information on shark attacks and a new rig 'Colossus' digging for oil. And that's it.

Awfully Good character: All of the characters in Megalodon are quite boring and each actor could play any of the roles with little to no difference to the film. So, by default, the shark will have to take this accolade.

Awfully Good line: Nothing. No cheeky or clever one liners at all.

Awfully Good scene: At least there are a couple of Awfully Good scenes. When one character sees the shark grab a submarine with it's teeth, he is distraught as his friend is inside. He and his friends are on an iceberg while the 60ft shark has surfaced with the sub in its mouth. But this doesn't stop him running towards the shark to save his friend. Other characters stop him unfortunately, because I wanted to see exactly what he was going to do to save the situation. Punching a 60ft shark on the nose probably wont work.

Other notes and scenes: Considering the director has worked in visual effects it's surprising that this film has some of the worst CGI you will ever see. And there's so much of it. Every scene seems to have CGI. Be it, the background, the submarine, the helicopter, the rig, the shark. Everything. The first sight of blood is when a small fish bites a guy. There's lots of blood but it's hard to see what's going on as the camera just shows super close-ups of the action. It takes almost an hour into the film for the viewer to see the shark. And the shark then head butts a submarine a bit before destroying it with his teeth. The second submarine soon goes downhill in the aforementioned Awfully Good scene. The shark then bursts through the iceberg and eats a stranded guy. Just before the final scene, the helicopter has the least dramatic crash, killing just the pilot.

Final scene: After not being able to save his friend, the guy decides he'll go into a submarine and get the shark himself. He just rams the sub into the shark a few times before it starts to chase him. Leading to an uneventful chase scene involving the shark being shot at with gas and then some kind of harpoon into its mouth. This leads to both of them crashing and a big poorly CGI'ed explosion. At first, it seems that the shark has just disappeared into thin air. But soon after we the shark in two halves fall to the bottom of the ocean. But that's not the end! Three months later the lead female is seen sailing alone and as the camera pans away we see, in the sea beneath, a giant shark!

Final thoughts: Not a lot happens in Megalodon. It's way too uneventful to be a good Awfully Good film. There are plenty of better giant shark films for you to enjoy.

DEAD SUSHI (2012)

'The Sushi Bites Back!'

Synopsis: Keiko, the daughter of a legendary sushi chef, runs away from home when his Karate-style regimen becomes too severe. Finding work at a rural hot springs inn, she is ridiculed by the eccentric staff and guests.

Director: Noburo Iguchi segment in the original ABCs of Death is called F is for Fart, so you should know what you're getting with him. Along with Dead Sushi he's directed a host of movies that will be in Volume 2 of Awfully Good Movies, including Zombie Ass: The Toilet of the Dead, Mutant Girls Squad, Robo-Geisha and The Machine Girl.

Cast: Main girl Rina Takeda has appeared in other great titled films such as, High-Kick Girl!, Karate Girl, The Kunoichi: Ninja Girl and Danger Dolls. Kentaro Shimazu starred in the quite well known and ridiculous but great titles, The Machine Girl and Tokyo Gore Police. Asami also appeared in The Machine Girl and Gun Woman. Aswell as some horribly titled films like the five film franchise, Rape Zombie: Lust of the Dead. But also the fantastically titled Your Mom is a Bitch! and Zombie Ass: Toilet of the Dead. Takashi Nishina starred in a segment of The ABCs of Death and more films with great titles; Godzilla, Mothra and King Ghidorah: Giant Monsters All-Out Attack, Horny House of Horror and Banana, Gloves and Whale Shark. Finally Yui Murata appeared in the ABCs of Death segment "F is for Fart" and Mutant Girls Squad.

Opening scene: Not too exciting. A young woman is taught by her father how to make the perfect sushi. This includes some karate somehow. But unfortunately she doesn't meet her father's standards and runs away to work in a sushi restaurant.

Awfully Good character: This has to be the homeless guy who is the cause of the man-eating sushi outbreak. His favourite 'weapon' is a large squid which he throws at people. This squid can fly though and do some serious damage to its victims! He also turns into a giant fish-human! But more on that later.....

Awfully Good line: *"I don't give a rats ass about my life. But i'm not gonna let you get away with wasting good food!"*. And why would you! Of course, this comes from the fish-human before he was part fish. There are many great lines that don't quite work when written down.

Awfully Good scene: So many to choose from! I'm going to go with the hilarious but slightly disturbing 'Japanese kiss' scene. This kiss involves an egg yolk being passed between the mouths of the couple kissing, several times. Dropping the yolk into each others mouths. It's as disturbing and weird as it sounds.

Other notes and scenes: The first death scene is pretty awesome. Homeless guy sets his squid free towards a young couple. The squid manages to decapitate the girl and her head flies through the air landing at the face of the guy as he embraces it with a kiss. As this happens the squid follows and spears itself through both heads, killing the guy aswell. There's actually some very good martial arts scenes. Usually with plenty of comedy thrown in. Rina Takeda is obviously very good at martial arts and the first fight we see is between her and six guys. One guy ends up naked and tied to the girl with a robe she is using to fight with.

Bits of sushi throughout the film bite at peoples bodies, faces, necks and everywhere else with blood spurting everywhere! One scene sees a woman's eyes pop out completely from her face. Another guy get his face beautifully but painfully looking, stretched from each side until the skin is ripped off - not dissimilar to a scene from Hellraiser. The squid was the culprit here again.

There's a character called Mr Egg, who is an egg and rice sushi. He can talk and has emotions and is the only 'good' dead sushi.

The flying sushi always look Awfully Good. Eventually some of the humans turn into zombies. We can see they are zombies because they have rice around there mouths. The scene when the guy turns into a human-fish is obviously fantastic and from then on we get an evil human-fish running about with an axe trying to kill people. He manages to decapitate someone giving a woman a shower of blood. Sushi nunchucks come into play. Because obviously. Fish-human throws up a sushi battleship that fires at the main girl and Mr Egg sacrifices itself to defeat the ship. That's a sentence I never thought I'd write.

Final scene: It all comes down to the big fight between Keiko (Takeda) and fish-human. It's a pretty great-looking fight scene and she defeats him by kicking him through a window and into the sky, where he explodes. She then returns to her father and becomes the ultimate sushi chef she was destined to be!

Final thoughts: Films don't get much more bizarre or strange as Dead Sushi. They also don't get much more fun. Asian directors seem to do these weird films the best. And I guess it's no surprise the director here Noboru Iguchi has directed many a strange movie. So if a film about zombie sushi sounds good to you, then Dead Sushi is perfect. But really any horror fan looking for something fun should check it out!

SPACE SHARKS (AKA RAGING SHARKS) (2005)

'You can swim, but you can't hide'

Synopsis: After debris from an alien spaceship lands in the waters, great white sharks begin terrorizing marine researchers in the Pacific Ocean.

Director: This is one of three shark movies from director Danny Lerner. The others being Shark Zone and Shark In Venice. He is better known as a producer, in which, he has worked on films such as The Expendables 2 & 3 and Olympus Has Fallen.

Cast: Corin Nemec gets the lead male role. His main roles have come in TV shows such as Supernatural and Stargate SG-1 but he also fought off sharks again in Sand Sharks! He still regularly works in films and shows you probably haven't seen. Vanessa Angel is the lead female. I'm not sure exactly what happened to her career. After wowing people in Weird Science and Kingpin she hasn't done too much else of note.
Corbin Bernsen has featured predominantly in the TV series Psych and also had a part in Kiss Kiss Bang Bang. Most recently he has featured in the show The Resident. Todd Jensen has had parts in Wrong Turn 3: Left for Dead and Mega Snake. Julian Vergov appeared in two other shark films, Shark Hunter and Shark Zone. Michael P. Flannigan has only made six acting appearances, this being his first but he has gone on to be producer in films such as Pitch Perfect and 88 Minutes. When I worked as a projectionist at a cinema, a book was kept of all the best names that popped up when we watched the end credits. I'm sure Binky van Bilderbeek would have been in there but unfortunately he has only appeared in eight films and only two films since 2011. Elise Muller also featured in SharkMan and the amazingly titled Vampire Lesbian

Kickboxers (I need to see that one)!

Opening scene: There's an opening shot of a spaceship. The CGI is actually not too bad. Then we see some pretty cool looking aliens speaking in, I assume, their own language. There's a crash and an explosion (there will be many more of these) and a pod flies down from space landing on Earth. Well to be exact, a boat, causing another big explosion with people flying off of the boats in time for the opening credits to roll.

Awfully Good character: Interesting characters were few and far between here. But Ben Stiles played by Todd Jensen gets the nod. He starts off as an annoying government health and safety inspector of some sort but turns out in a (not so) shocking twist to be part of the Black Ops. I'm not really sure how he got to where he is but they found out eventually. He's a pretty unexciting and unconvincing as bad guys go. But at least he does meet a glorious end.

Awfully Good line: Just two words. *"Bloody hell"*. It amused me more than it should have and is definitely not used enough. It just beat *"Damn magnetic spikes"*. Which I think is better left unexplained.

Awfully Good scene: I'm going with the ridiculousness of the scene in which it is decided that torpedoing the sharks is the best option. Despite that there is a diver nearby and that, well sharks move about a lot. Surely it wouldn't be that easy?! Well, actually it seems it is, as it nearly works. There's a lot of explosions and the guy doesn't die.

Other notes and scenes: Space Sharks features two things very heavily. People on computers from what looks like the eighties, and explosions. The first isn't that exciting so I'll write about the second. Sharks bite some kind of electrical cords and sparks fly, as they do when they attack a TV news crew's boat. The submarines seem to have explosions inside them almost constantly. Near the start of the film, two divers are attacked by sharks, so one guy decides to go out and help. When they also get into some trouble, another guy offers to go out and help. It seems many of the characters have a death wish. Vanessa Angel's character at one point starts shouting at a guy that won't fix something in the water because the sharks are out there. But when her husband offers to do it, she is not happy at all! Even threatening to kill the other guy. The sharks take a break from attacking the crew at the start to go to Bermuda and attack some surfers and girls in bikinis instead. Two people literally get stabbed in the back. The first one dies but Awfully Good favourite Stiles, barely flinched when it happens to him. He just pulled the knife out of his back and carried on as normal. He does eventually act injured when an arrow is shot in his back. All of the shark attacks actually look quite good, although a lot of them are really close-up and hard to see. Some of it seems to be stock footage of actual sharks and it's used quite well. The main story by the way, involving the aliens, is about some orange crystal-like energy source that the sharks are defending for the aliens, who eventually come back to collect it.

Final scene: The married couple are the only survivors on the destroyed submarine but have no way to escape. They watch out of a window as the aliens return in their spaceship underwater and collect the orange stuff. There is then a massive explosion where it is assumed the couple are dead. But, of course they are not. They are alive and start banging on the side of a rescue submarine and are let in! Stiles also manages to survive. But while he is in the sea escaping, a shark comes along and decapitates him nicely, turning the water red. Finishing with a happy end for most.

Final thoughts: Space Sharks was not as an exciting concept as the title might suggest. But it's not too bad a film. Despite maybe taken itself a little too seriously, it still manages to be quite fun.

SNAKEHEAD SWAMP (2014)

*'When you're in the Bayou,
you're dead in the water'*

Synopsis: In the quiet swamps of the Louisiana bayou, what started as an exciting boating trip will soon end up in a bloodbath, when genetically altered snake-fish infest the river.

Director: It's Don E. FauntLeRoy again. He that directed Damn Sea Vampires!

Cast: Ayla Kell has appeared in a few TV shows including Weeds, Malcom in the Middle and CSI Miami but her last role was in 2021 with two interestingly titled movies - Pizza and Whine and Terror Eyes. Antonio Fargas is best known for playing Huggy Bear in the Starsky and Hutch TV show. Dave Davis has some horror on his CV with an episode of The Walking Dead, American Horror House, Leprechaun's Revenge, Ozark Sharks and the recent Nic Cage Dracula flick Renfield. Melissa Cordero had a minor role in 21 Jump Street as 'Naked Drama Threesome'??!! And appeared in 2014 comedy horror Ghost of Goodnight Lane. Ross Britz had a small role in a recent episode of American Horror Story, while also appearing in Ozark Sharks, aswell as Shark Island and an episode of The Purge. Sloane Coe only has five credits in her acting career but all horror ones! Ghost Shark, Devil's Due, Snakehead Swamp, Shark Island and Proof of the Devil 2. Danny Cosmo has had a few small roles in horror films including Monsterwolf and 13 Sins but most importantly he appeared in the fantastic Santa Jaws. Peaches Davis's first role was in 2012's The Campaign and has only had a few small roles since.

Opening scene: The opening moments show parts of two different scenes. One involving a guy taking part in some kind of ritual that involved chickens being chopped up with a knife and lots of blood spraying everywhere. The other featuring a cargo van carrying (we assume) Snakeheads. The van crashes into a nearby swamp and its contents kill the driver and passenger. The guy doing the ritual announces "It's started", just incase you weren't sure.

Awfully Good character: Marge played by Peaches Davis is the almost perfect Awfully good character. She works as at the local police station, seemingly just to answer the phone. But her one job she can't do because she's deaf and her hearing aid needs fixing. But they continue to employ her anyway. Thankfully she's not completely useless because as we discover later, hand her a gun and she's pretty handy with it. It's a great image seeing an elderly woman holding a big gun, shooting at a snake/fish hybrid.

Awfully Good line: When one character is unsure how to use a gun, his ex-wife explains. ***"Aim this at the man-eating killer fish and then pull this."*** I've never used a gun but it seems pretty simple to me based on that advice.

Awfully Good scene: It was only really a brief moment but seeing the elderly Marge holding a massive powerful gun and firing several shots at the Snakehead fish thing and killing it, was a wonderful sight!

Other notes and scenes: The first proper sight we get of the snake fish is when it drags away a police officer, kills him, and his colleague, with plenty of blood splatter added. A lot of the deaths are basically the same but with different characters. Someone falls or is dragged into the water, there's lots of splashing about, they get dragged under and the water around that area turns red with blood. The police were wonderfully panicky at one point, shooting randomly at the water when one person got dragged in. I quite liked the scene watched through CCTV as the snake fish roams through a nearby park, killing people along the way.
The father goes crazy on a small snake fish at one point. Killing it with a cleaver, hitting it again and again and covering his nice white shirt with blood. One character suggests they might be "psycho fish from space", now that's a title! Snakehead Swamp actually has a couple of moments I really liked. One stabbing through a door to the character you will dislike the most and another face to face moment between man and snake fish. Marge kills again and no-one bats an eye lid. I guess everyone already knew she was awesome with a gun. Which makes me wonder why they

didn't get her involved sooner. There's what seems like every love story possible involved here. A guy and girl where the guy is a bit of an idiot. And then another guy that has always liked that girl. There's a mother and son relationship that is on/off, and an about to be divorced couple who might get back together.

Final scene: A girl gets a cut on her leg after she is bitten by a snake fish. She needs to go hospital apparently but it really doesn't look so bad.
Because the situation has got so serious, it seems the national guard are just going to bomb the swamp. But our heroes will hopefully do something before that happens. They travel down the swamp via boat being chased by a giant snake fish. They just look kind of like a giant slug fish, not that scary really. But anyway, it appears they can move quick. They continue shooting at it once on land, including Marge again. She literally has to be dragged away and told to go. The final end of the giant snake fish is a little underwhelming. They keep shooting at it, eventually chuck some alcohol at it, and fire a flare gun towards it. Therefore creating some kind of fire bomb, burning it to the ground. Of course, all the couples get together and there's a happy ending for everybody.

Final thoughts: SnakeHead Swamp is a pretty entertaining film in the Awfully Good genre. There's plenty of entertaining characters, fun scenes and poor CGI. If you enjoy most of SyFy's offerings, you'll enjoy this.

GHOSTQUAKE (AKA HAUNTED HIGH) (2012)

'Showing your school spirit can be deadly'

Synopsis: When Halloman Academy, a posh New England private school, is visited by a demonic headmaster, a humble janitor, who is secretly the guardian of the school, teams up with the headmaster's grandson in order to save the academy.

Director: Jeffrey Scott Lando also has House of Bones, Roboshark and Boogeyman to his name.

Cast: Charisma Carpenter, yep, Cordelia from Buffy and Angel, makes a brief appearance. Danny Trejo (Machete, From Dusk Til Dawn) makes a slightly longer appearance. If only his character was a bit more like Machete! Jonathan Baron starred in two episodes of True Blood, played Dr. Heart in Doom Patrol and most recently starred in Netflix's holiday rom-com Holidate. Gabe Begneaud has appeared in an episode of True Detective and American Horror Story: Coven, aswell as playing 'Deputy Jordan' in the excellent American Ultra. Marc Donato was apparently 'nodding 1st grader' in Billy Madison. M.C. Gainey has many acting credits, including Django Unchained, 18 episodes of Lost as Tom Friendly, Hank in Club Dread and Swamp Thing in Con Air. Griff Furst has starred in Monsterwolf, Atomic Shark and Boa vs Python but would probably prefer to be known for his work in films such as Focus and The Founder. Dana Gourrier has appeared in several episodes of both American Horror Story: Coven and True Detective. She also appeared in Django Unchained, The Hateful Eight and the recent Interview With the Vampire series. Mike Kimmel has acted in films with such titles as Flying Monkeys and Killer Tumbleweeds. Brett Lapeyrouse has been a part of the remake of Oldboy and 21 Jump Street. Jaren Mitchell starred in horror remake the Town That Dreaded Sundown and another Awfully Good favourite, Ghost Shark. He also played Doug Vargas in nine episodes of The Purge. Shawn C. Phillips has starred in many Awfully Good films including Jersey Shore Massacre, Sheriff Tom vs the Zombies and Camp Massacre but he's recently started directing more. His directorial efforts include segments in many horror anthologies and Amityville Karen. Lastly, Lauren Pennington has one other horror on her C.V. - the long winded title, The Haunting in Connecticut 2: Ghosts of Georgia. Oh, and Sharknado director Anthony C. Ferrante co-wrote Ghostquake.

Opening scene: It's very long winded. At least five minutes passes with not a whole lot of interest happening. Eventually a teacher, Myers, tells a student, Quentin, he is needed in the basement. He doesn't ask why, just follows. They have a bit of an argument about Quentin's family history and then some gold coins he has on him get knocked to the floor. This somehow starts a small earthquake which lets out some ghosts from a time capsule!? It's as ridiculous as it sounds.

Awfully Good character: There's a few I could choose. I'm going with Blake played by Shawn C. Phillips. Here's the overweight geek who is good on computers and watches too much TV. Here, he is given the worst dialogue. He has a much higher pitched voice than you expect, which adds to the comedy, and despite being picked on a lot for most the film, here's not particularly likeable. Unfortunately his death is kind of boring.

Awfully Good line: There's quite a few to choose from. But after a character is found dead, someone asks **"What do you mean Kimberley's dead?". "She has no head."** That covers it well and no more explanation was needed.

Awfully Good scene: If I said zombie frogs, I'm sure you'll understand why it's my favourite scene. The ghostly spirits somehow bring science class frogs back to life and they attack two teachers. Luckily there's a scalpel and Bunsen burner nearby and the principal, rather aggressively kills off the frogs. He's very proud of himself about it to.

Other notes and scenes: The few earthquake, or I guess, ghostquake, scenes are people falling off things in a very staged-looking way as the camera shakes about a bit. Danny Trejo is pretty badly miscast as the janitor. He is not very tough, even getting beat up by a high school girl. These are some clever ghosts that even managed to get into peoples mobile phones and on their computers. There's no escaping them. One girl follows who she thinks is the teacher, into the shower. After he doesn't reply to her, she thinks it's best to just strip off and join him in the shower. It's not a great plan and she only gets her tie off before she's killed. The main ghost, the old principal, has an assistant ghost. She looks awful, with bad make-up (a stuck on yellow nose) and awful CGI. One guy is described as "extra crispy" instead of dead. One scene includes green slime on the floor that means our characters can't move. The goo reminded me of Slimer from Ghostbusters. Flying football shirts help kill one guy, as he is tied to some gym equipment and killed. I'm not sure how exactly because we don't get to see. I was introduced to a new word.....polterbush! Being ambushed by a poltergeist apparently. One girl has her neck broken via trumpet! Charisma Carpenter shows up for about one minute and is killed by the ghost assistant. She appears as a librarian and sinks into the library floor. At one point the ghost wears an old knights armour to attack. I'm not really sure why.

Final scene: Well, a lot seems to happen. The principal ghost has magical powers where he shoots green electrical strikes from his hands! His assistant starts crawling to our
survivors. But she is stopped by the ghost of Danny Trejo's sister. It's not her first appearance in the film. The principal also has some spells he chants out to help him. The only way to win is by our survivors pouring acid over the gold coins from the first scene. This leads to the line "Acid's a bad trip!". The ghost then 'enters' his grandson and takes over his body. Danny Trejo kept calling out to him by saying some spell but this didn't help and he is killed. There's another ghostquake and the girl our main guy is trying to get with, kisses him, which somehow breaks the fact that his grandfathers ghost is controlling him. But the ghost comes back again only for Danny Trejo to return as a topless ghost, an unknown reason, and help 'pull' the ghost out of the body. At some point, someone gets the acid and melts the coins down and that's pretty much how things end.

Final thoughts: Ghostquake is so Awfully Good, ridiculous and random it's hard not to raise a smile while watching it.

DAMN SEA VAMPIRES! (2013)

'Here comes deep shit'

Synopsis: With their father killed by a swarm of vampiric sea creatures, Bering Sea adventurers, Joe and Donna, team up with a marine biologist and her devoted deckhand to render the species extinct.

Director: The Fantastically named director Don E. FauntLeRoy also directed Snakehead Swamp (as previously mentioned), Anacondas: Trail of Blood and Anaconda: The Offspring.

Cast: Cassandra Scerbo is the lead female here and I thought she'd go on to bigger things but it seems she will be known for her role in the Sharknado films. Brandon Beemer hasn't done a whole lot of movie work but has worked on 484 episodes of Days of Our Lives and 43 episodes of The Bay. Jaqueline Fleming has horror credits with Abraham Lincoln: Vampire Hunter, a single episode of The Walking Dead and Vegas Vampires. Jonathan Lipnicki will probably always be known for being George Little in the Stuart Little films. Lastly, Lawrence Turner has featured in Dallas Buyers Club, RED, Mirrors 2 and the Benson and Moorhead movie Synchronic.

Opening scene: Not as dramatic as normal for Awfully Good and it's dragged out a bit. But eventually a group of people go diving, only to unearth some creatures in the sea bed below. One of the crew is attacked and killed by the sea vampire. Once the other diver is back on the boat, the rest are chased by the creature but they all escape.

Awfully Good character: The villain of the piece is the highlight. 'Thorne' played by Lawrence Turner is not that evil for the main villain. He dresses like a cowboy, complete with moustache and has a sidekick, Jimmy, who is always on screen with him but I don't think ever utters a word. He ends up working with the good guys, after telling Jimmy to hurt or possibly kill everyone else but of course is killed by the sea vampires.

Awfully Good line: Sadly another one of these movies that needs to work on its quotability. Nothing of note!

Awfully Good scene: Damn Sea Vampires! has its own little homage to Aliens. The father of the family (who is seemingly uncredited despite being in the film quite a lot) is attacked by a sea vampire and he is stabbed in the chest. This somehow produces the spawn inside him. He is being driven to the hospital when he frantically thrashes about with everyone around him, when out pops a sea vampire from his chest, splashing blood all over the car windows.

Other notes and scenes: Firstly, apparently nobody tells the police about anything. Ever. When the crew's first member is killed, the rest decide to say nothing until after an important auction they have. They still don't mention it after the auction. Another person, a scientist finds the body washed up the next day. Does she tell the police? Of course not! She tells the crew that she has the body but explains to them they and the police cant have it until she has run some tests on it. And for the rest of the film, through many deaths and explosions, the police are never thought of really. They briefly mention no-one can reach them because of a storm but I'm not having it.
A guy gets dragged into the sea at one point just because he wont let go of his fishing rod. Here's screaming and panicking about going in but still doesn't feel the need to let go. Several times the sea vampires seem to cuddle their prey to death. They wrap the wings around them and then eat them in an unconvincing way. At one point a guy perfectly runs over one with a lorry and then dumps some sand on it, burying it all in one quick move. George Little is dragged on to an electric fence, which doesn't end well. One scene just came runner-up for 'Awfully Good scene'. A guy drives off on a motorbike but a sea vampire is soon after him and decapitating him in one quick swoop. A headless body continues going and seemingly explodes for no good reason! Infact, things blow up and set fire to themselves quite regularly. The brother of the family is shown to be a traitor quite early on but no-one ever finds out. This might seem

minor but his betrayal eventually leads to his father's death and he gets no comeuppance for that at all. The sea vampires themselves look quite cool. But when interacting with anything the CGI looks pretty bad. Of course they are sensitive to light (they are vampires remember) and this leads to their ultimate demise. Oh, and they do seem to change in size at different times. I don't mean some are small and some are large. I mean one can be small at one point and large at others. This isn't a trick they do, just bad effects (I'm used to that now with this films to be honest).

Final scene: The remaining people set-up a pretty elaborate plan. Their main weapon being light guns! They're not really guns, they just look like them. And they 'shoot' beams of light towards the vampires, killing them instantly in a big explosion. I guess they are more powerful than the lights they have at first because it initially took a bit of time for them to explode and die. Of course, it takes a big explosion to kill them all. This happens a lot in Awfully Good films. And one nicely set-up UV explosion does the trick.

Final thoughts: Damn Sea Vampires! is a pretty fun film. The creatures are ridiculous but kind of great. It's somehow not quite cheesy enough but even when trying to be serious it's still enjoyable.

ATTACK OF THE VEGAN ZOMBIES (2010)

'Zero trans fats have never been so deadly'

Synopsis: Joe and his wife Dionne have had yet another bad crop for their winery. Faced with the prospect of losing the family farm, Dionne convinces her mother (a witch) to cast a spell upon next year's crop. The crop is such a success that Joe hires some college students to help them harvest. However, when a nosy neighbour begins poking around in the fields, he finds out more than he bargained for. Now the question isn't how to best harvest the crop, it's how to keep from being harvested!

Director: Jim Townsend also plays one of the central roles in the film and it's the only film he has directed.

Cast: Kerry Kearns seems to enjoy starring in horror, she also featured in Zombthology, Zombie Armageddon and Cannibal Cheerleader Camp. Natalie Jablokov also played a zombie in the film Shadow: Dead Riot, whose lead was played by Tony Todd. Mike Shiflett's next film was 2012's Lincoln. Ames Arnold appeared in another interestingly titled film, Massacre at Buffalo Valley. Charisse Matthews has uncredited roles in Men In Black 3 and the TV show 30 Rock. Unsurprisingly, several actors have a few or, no other roles to their name.

Opening scene: There's a guy walking through a vineyard and not much is growing. We see some close-ups of dead birds then a guy trying some wine. There's some eerie music but not a lot else.

Awfully Good character: Well ,there's two. They are best friends and nerds. It's a stereotypical character but it works well in certain types of films. Generally ones that don't take themselves too seriously. The two actors play the roles well, a bit like Napoleon Dynamite but not quite as cool.

Awfully Good line: There was actually a few to choose from and this one comes from the nerds when they debate whether they can 'get with' the two girls. *"They're party girls genetically programmed to party."*

Awfully Good scene: If I'm honest it takes a while for the really fun scenes to start to happen. It's the first sight of a zombie when a character named Fred appears looking a bit unwell. The make-up actually isn't too bad and the camera shakes about to make up for it. Out of nowhere the zombie is decapitated in what is the first real act of violence in the film. Green goo rather than blood squirts from the neck.

Other notes and scenes: In a strange turn of events, the first killers are the vines. Yes, this is plants attacking people, no surprise really. There's also a witch heavily involved in it all and of course the zombies. The zombies created from the vines. The vines and zombies go after the humans because they want or need wine or grapes. And apparently the characters in this film drink enough that wine is in their blood at a high level. These killer vines are clever enough that they take out phone lines and destroy car engines. The most ridiculous scene in the whole film involves the two main young women. One of them suddenly starts crying and blaming herself for stuff that has happened. And then, the other girl starts coming on to her. They are soon getting naked and kiss and then we see them wake up in bed together. I think the whole scene happens just so a joke can be told a bit later. I'm pretty sure every character wore the same clothes throughout the whole film. And it lasts more than a day for them all. Actually on second thoughts, that's pretty normal. Once people are infected, things get crazier. A vine comes from one woman's mouth like a tongue, people turn green when they are zombified, and one girl cartwheels her way into a fight.

Final scene: We discover the zombies must be killed with a potion from the witch. They get a cauldron over a fire, mix together some wine to lure them and then chuck the zombies in the fire. Another zombie gets his head crushed in grape crushing machine and then the final one is killed when it somehow suffers a stake through the heart. I say somehow because the piece of wood looked very blunt. Finally, we see a news reporter talking about the missing people and the one survivor who is now pregnant. It turns out though that the news reporter is a zombie.

Final thoughts: Attack of the Vegan Zombies is almost as much fun as the title suggests. It far exceeded my expectations. It knew it was a silly b-movie but the acting was actually at a decent level. It's an absolutely ridiculous idea but it works and I enjoyed it. Something a bit different for a zombie film is nearly always needed.

BIRDEMIC: SHOCK AND TERROR (2010)

'Who will survive'

Synopsis: A horde of mutated birds descends upon the quiet town of Half Moon Bay, California. As the death toll rises, two citizens manage to fight back, but will they survive Birdemic?

Director: James Nguyen directed a couple of films before this and went on to make Birdemic 2: Resurrection and Birdemic 3: Sea Eagle. Neither of which I have seen yet.

Cast: Apart from the Birdemic films, Alan Bagh's claim to fame until recently was a deleted scene in Ghost Shark 2: Urban Jaws. But last year he appeared in three episodes of The Book of Boba Fett! Whitney Moore has starred in The Theatre Bizarre,
Contracted: Phase II, Santanic Panic, Evil Bong 888: Infinity High and Another Yet a Lover Story: Life on the Streets. Adam Sessa also appeared in Chastity Bites. Rick Camp has uncredited roles in Patch Adams, Four Christmases and The Pursuit of Happyness. And John Grant appeared in Hobgoblins 2. Unsurprisingly a lot of the cast have only starred in the two or three Birdemic films or only acted in one or two more.

Opening scene: Well there isn't really much of one. What we get is a camera inside a car while it drives along and the opening credits role. And that's it.

Awfully Good character: There's also not much in the way of characters. But we do get 'tree hugger'. I don't remember his name to be honest and he's only briefly in the film but one of the children in the film calls him a tree hugger. This is because he lives in a (CGI) treehouse in the forest. He talks about how the eagles don't attack people there and how humans are the real threat and that the trees will be gone in a 'few' years. He leaves the film because he can hear a mountain lion, so makes a quick exit.

Awfully Good line: This was another hard one to pick out because all the best lines are said seriously and wouldn't seem so funny written down. But I did like *"why can't we just give peace a chance?"*. It's after a chat about the Iraq war but I think applies nicely to birds to.

Awfully Good scene: The eagles are attacking and our four main characters see a double decker bus at the side of the road being attacked. One guy, armed with a gun, goes to save the three people on board. He shoots a couple of eagles out of the sky and gets inside the bus but no-one wants to leave. He just forces them to anyway, although they don't put up much of a fight. Once they are out of the bus the eagles attack again and they either take a crap on the four characters or they are sick on them. I'm not sure which. This liquid though, puts its victims in a lot of pain as they scream and fall to the floor. Once there, they are open to be killed off by the eagles.

Other notes and scenes: Where to start?! Well to be honest, not a lot happens for the first 47 minutes. That's the time we first see any sign of eagles killing humans and it is all of a sudden like a bird apocalypse. In this 47 minutes you realise how bad this film is. The acting is wooden and terrible, the script and especially the unnatural dialogue is awful, while the music is annoying and repetitive. Perhaps the worst part of it all is the editing, particularly on the sound. Whether it be different background noises on the same scene. Or background noise so loud you can't hear the actors speaking. Or music and dialogue just cutting out as the scene changes. There's many many scenes where nothing much happens. Driving in a car, people walking and watching TV, just mundane things that aren't needed but take up half the run time. I haven't mentioned the eagles themselves too much. They are CGI (if you hadn't guessed) and the effects are so bad that I'd be annoyed if they were in a film made in the 1970s. This was made in 2010! My second favourite scene involved our two main characters dancing in a bar to a live singer. Not only are they seemingly the only two people in the bar and therefore being personally sung to but neither of them can dance at all! Before our characters have guns, which seem to appear from thin air, their weapon of choice is coat hangers. One of my favourite moments of the film is a five second close-up on some trees like they are some kind of character. One of the most ridiculous things in the film is the stupidity of the characters. The prime example is that after discovering there are killer eagles taking over the place, they decide to spend a lot of time outdoors in wide open spaces. Fields, the beach, anywhere easily accessible for birds. The director also has some environmental agenda which he tells you about for the whole film.

Final scene: After cooking some fish and seaweed and it being rejected by the kids ("I want a Happy Meal!"), the eagles attack! The two adults and two children run back to their van that is out of petrol. And to make matters worse, they are out of bullets too. One eagle flies head first into the windscreen but dies on impact. And then suddenly the eagles just stop and fly away. Yes, like a lot of the film, a poor copy of the classic horror The Birds. The four survivors stand on the beach and watch the birds fly away.

Final thoughts: I've always said to anybody that will listen, that a SyFy-style film involving killer eagles could be great. Just look on YouTube for videos of eagles attacking other animals. It's scary! Unfortunately, Birdemic isn't that film. There's just enough Awfully Good moments to keep you interested and this is perhaps THE so bad it's good film. But at the same time it's almost impossible to recommend it.

AFTERWORD

Thank you for purchasing and reading this book. If you enjoyed it could you please spend five minutes reviewing it on amazon, goodreads or wherever else you review your books! It would be greatly appreciated.

ABOUT THE AUTHOR

Alain Elliott

Author of 'Home Sweet Home: A Horror Anthology', 'Twas the Night Before Christmas and Everyone Was Dying, and Wight of the Living Dead. Alain Elliott also writes for Nerdly and several other sites covering horror, retro gaming and everything in between, while also the creator of horror blog 'Wight Blood'.

BOOKS BY THIS AUTHOR

Home Sweet Home: A Horror Anthology

Home Sweet Home is a horror anthology featuring five terrifying tales based around different rooms in the home.

A bedroom is the location for a heart to heart between grandmother and granddaughter until one of them needs their demons exorcised.

Christmas is that happy, joyous time of year for family gatherings but in this dining room, the Christmas dinner turns nasty as one family member seems unable to control their violent tendencies.

What happens when your kitchen appliances come to life and try to murder you? This family will soon find out when the blender left in their new home sets out to kill them all.

A newly married couple has found the perfect home. Size, location, and price all seem too good to be true. There is a catch of course and that catch is what's living in the attic.

After a night out, two friends discover their local neighbourhood has been taken over by zombies. They end up stuck in their bathroom with seemingly no escape from the undead waiting on the other side of the door.

These five spine-chilling stories will show that there really is no place like home.

Wight Of The Living Dead

Ryan's life has been going down hill slowly ever since he left the Isle of Wight twenty years ago. The move to Portsmouth was supposed to be a positive one. A new life for him to start. But that's not what happened.

It was now six years since he had lasted visited his friends and family on the island, but he needed a break. With a rusty camper van and hopes of reliving the best memories of his childhood, initially, the Isle of Wight seemed like a good idea. But, when he wakes up to a beach full of dead sea creatures, and the only people he sees are trying to kill him, he remembers why he left in the first place.

But now his family's life are at risk, he must help them escape the island alongside him

'Twas The Night Before Christmas And Everyone Was Dying

Christmas has come early with this selection of six short horror stories set on Christmas Eve!

Four friends meet every Christmas Eve in an empty field on the outskirts of town but one of them has discovered that there might be something sinister nearby. Will they survive the night?

Christmas Eve and Daryl wakes up with a pounding headache. Is it simply a hangover or are those dreams of reindeer important? A violent and gory few hours later gives him the answer.

Who wants to be stood in a freezing school playground on Christmas Eve shouting at misbehaved kids? Not Kevin, who soon finds out that this cold weather can be deadly.

Singing Christmas carols to their neighbours seems like easy money to two best friends. But when their elderly neighbour only has chocolate to give them, their decision to punish her might be the last one they make.

The residents of a small hamlet are fed up with their festive season being ruined every year, and have decided to take matters into their own, bloody, hands.

Santa gets a surprise when the children he is delivering to are awake and waiting for him. They want more than just presents.

Christmas folklore and tradition blend nicely together in this original collection of Christmas horror that features Santa Claus, Elves, giant Christmas trees, perfectly decorated houses and as much snow as there is blood (lots!).

Printed in Great Britain
by Amazon